MongoDB Applied Design Patterns

Rick Copeland

O'REILLY®

Beijing · Cambridge · Farnham · Köln · Sebastopol · Tokyo

MongoDB Applied Design Patterns

by Rick Copeland

Printed in the United States of America.

Published by O'Reilly Media, Inc., 1005 Gravenstein Highway North, Sebastopol, CA 95472.

O'Reilly books may be purchased for educational, business, or sales promotional use. Online editions are also available for most titles (*http://my.safaribooksonline.com*). For more information, contact our corporate/institutional sales department: 800-998-9938 or *corporate@oreilly.com*.

Editors: Mike Loukides and Meghan Blanchette
Production Editor: Kristen Borg
Copyeditor: Kiel Van Horn
Proofreader: Jasmine Kwityn

Indexer: Jill Edwards
Cover Designer: Karen Montgomery
Interior Designer: David Futato
Illustrator: Kara Ebrahim

March 2013:   First Edition

Revision History for the First Edition:

2013-03-01:   First release

See *http://oreilly.com/catalog/errata.csp?isbn=9781449340049* for release details.

ISBN: 978-1-449-34004-9

[LSI]

Table of Contents

Preface

Whether you're building the newest and hottest social media website or developing an internal-use-only enterprise business intelligence application, scaling your data model has never been more important. Traditional relational databases, while familiar, present significant challenges and complications when trying to scale up to such "big data" needs. Into this world steps MongoDB, a leading NoSQL database, to address these scaling challenges while also simplifying the process of development.

However, in all the hype surrounding big data, many sites have launched their business on NoSQL databases without an understanding of the techniques necessary to effectively use the features of their chosen database. This book provides the much-needed connection between the features of MongoDB and the business problems that it is suited to solve. The book's focus on the practical aspects of the MongoDB implementation makes it an ideal purchase for developers charged with bringing MongoDB's scalability to bear on the particular problem you've been tasked to solve.

Audience

This book is intended for those who are interested in learning practical patterns for solving problems and designing applications using MongoDB. Although most of the features of MongoDB highlighted in this book have a basic description here, this is not a beginning MongoDB book. For such an introduction, the reader would be well-served to start with *MongoDB: The Definitive Guide* by Kristina Chodorow and Michael Dirolf (O'Reilly) or, for a Python-specific introduction, *MongoDB and Python* by Niall O'Higgins (O'Reilly).

Assumptions This Book Makes

Most of the code examples used in this book are implemented using either the Python or JavaScript programming languages, so a basic familiarity with their syntax is essential to getting the most out of this book. Additionally, many of the examples and patterns are contrasted with approaches to solving the same problems using relational databases, so basic familiarity with SQL and relational modeling is also helpful.

Contents of This Book

This book is divided into two parts, with Part I focusing on general MongoDB design patterns and Part II applying those patterns to particular problem domains.

Part I: Design Patterns

Part I introduces the reader to some generally applicable design patterns in MongoDB. These chapters include more introductory material than Part II, and tend to focus more on MongoDB techniques and less on domain-specific problems. The techniques described here tend to make use of MongoDB distinctives, or generate a sense of "hey, MongoDB can't do that" as you learn that yes, indeed, it can.

Chapter 1: To Embed or Reference
> This chapter describes what kinds of documents can be stored in MongoDB, and illustrates the trade-offs between schemas that embed related documents within related documents and schemas where documents simply reference one another by ID. It will focus on the performance benefits of embedding, and when the complexity added by embedding outweighs the performance gains.

Chapter 2: Polymorphic Schemas
> This chapter begins by illustrating that MongoDB collections are schemaless, with the schema actually being stored in individual documents. It then goes on to show how this feature, combined with document embedding, enables a flexible and efficient polymorphism in MongoDB.

Chapter 3: Mimicking Transactional Behavior
> This chapter is a kind of apologia for MongoDB's lack of complex, multidocument transactions. It illustrates how MongoDB's modifiers, combined with document embedding, can often accomplish in a single atomic document update what SQL would require several distinct updates to achieve. It also explores a pattern for implementing an application-level, two-phase commit protocol to provide transactional guarantees in MongoDB when they are absolutely required.

Part II: Use Cases

In Part II, we turn to the "applied" part of *Applied Design Patterns*, showing several use cases and the application of MongoDB patterns to solving domain-specific problems. Each chapter here covers a particular problem domain and the techniques and patterns used to address the problem.

Chapter 4: Operational Intelligence

This chapter describes how MongoDB can be used for operational intelligence, or "real-time analytics" of business data. It describes a simple event logging system, extending that system through the use of periodic and incremental hierarchical aggregation. It then concludes with a description of a true real-time incremental aggregation system, the Mongo Monitoring Service (MMS), and the techniques and trade-offs made there to achieve high performance on huge amounts of data over hundreds of customers with a (relatively) small amount of hardware.

Chapter 5: Ecommerce

This chapter begins by describing how MongoDB can be used as a product catalog master, focusing on the polymorphic schema techniques and methods of storing hierarchy in MongoDB. It then describes an inventory management system that uses optimistic updating and compensation to achieve eventual consistency even without two-phase commit.

Chapter 6: Content Management Systems

This chapter describes how MongoDB can be used as a backend for a content management system. In particular, it focuses on the use of polymorphic schemas for storing content nodes, the use of GridFS and Binary fields to store binary assets, and various approaches to storing discussions.

Chapter 7: Online Advertising Networks

This chapter describes the design of an online advertising network. The focus here is on embedded documents and complex atomic updates, as well as making sure that the storage engine (MongoDB) never becomes the bottleneck in the ad-serving decision. It will cover techniques for frequency capping ad impressions, keyword targeting, and keyword bidding.

Chapter 8: Social Networking

This chapter describes how MongoDB can be used to store a relatively complex social graph, modeled after the Google+ product, with users in various circles, allowing fine-grained control over what is shared with whom. The focus here is on maintaining the graph, as well as categorizing content into various timelines and news feeds.

Chapter 9: Online Gaming

This chapter describes how MongoDB can be used to store data necessary for an online, multiplayer role-playing game. We show how character and world data can be stored in MongoDB, allowing for concurrent access to the same data structures from multiple players.

Conventions Used in This Book

The following typographical conventions are used in this book:

Italic

> Indicates new terms, URLs, email addresses, filenames, and file extensions.

`Constant width`

> Used for program listings, as well as within paragraphs to refer to program elements such as variable or function names, databases, data types, environment variables, statements, and keywords.

`Constant width bold`

> Shows commands or other text that should be typed literally by the user.

`Constant width italic`

> Shows text that should be replaced with user-supplied values or by values determined by context.

 This icon signifies a tip, suggestion, or general note.

 This icon indicates a warning or caution.

Using Code Examples

This book is here to help you get your job done. In general, if this book includes code examples, you may use the code in this book in your programs and documentation. You do not need to contact us for permission unless you're reproducing a significant portion of the code. For example, writing a program that uses several chunks of code from this book does not require permission. Selling or distributing a CD-ROM of examples from O'Reilly books does require permission. Answering a question by citing this book and quoting example code does not require permission. Incorporating a significant amount of example code from this book into your product's documentation does require permission.

We appreciate, but do not require, attribution. An attribution usually includes the title, author, publisher, and ISBN. For example: "*MongoDB Applied Design Patterns* by Rick Copeland (O'Reilly). Copyright 2013 Richard D. Copeland, Jr., 978-1-449-34004-9."

If you feel your use of code examples falls outside fair use or the permission given here, feel free to contact us at *permissions@oreilly.com*.

Safari® Books Online

 Safari Books Online is an on-demand digital library that delivers expert content in both book and video form from the world's leading authors in technology and business.

Technology professionals, software developers, web designers, and business and creative professionals use Safari Books Online as their primary resource for research, problem solving, learning, and certification training.

Safari Books Online offers a range of product mixes and pricing programs for organizations, government agencies, and individuals. Subscribers have access to thousands of books, training videos, and prepublication manuscripts in one fully searchable database from publishers like O'Reilly Media, Prentice Hall Professional, Addison-Wesley Professional, Microsoft Press, Sams, Que, Peachpit Press, Focal Press, Cisco Press, John Wiley & Sons, Syngress, Morgan Kaufmann, IBM Redbooks, Packt, Adobe Press, FT Press, Apress, Manning, New Riders, McGraw-Hill, Jones & Bartlett, Course Technology, and dozens more. For more information about Safari Books Online, please visit us online.

How to Contact Us

Please address comments and questions concerning this book to the publisher:

O'Reilly Media, Inc.
1005 Gravenstein Highway North
Sebastopol, CA 95472
800-998-9938 (in the United States or Canada)
707-829-0515 (international or local)
707-829-0104 (fax)

We have a web page for this book, where we list errata, examples, and any additional information. You can access this page at *http://oreil.ly/mongodb-applied-design-patterns*.

To comment or ask technical questions about this book, send email to *bookquestions@oreilly.com*.

For more information about our books, courses, conferences, and news, see our website at *http://www.oreilly.com*.

Find us on Facebook: *http://facebook.com/oreilly*

Follow us on Twitter: *http://twitter.com/oreillymedia*

Watch us on YouTube: *http://www.youtube.com/oreillymedia*

Acknowledgments

Many thanks go to O'Reilly's Meghan Blanchette, who endured the frustrations of trying to get a technical guy writing a book to come up with a workable schedule and stick to it. Sincere thanks also go to my technical reviewers, Jesse Davis and Mike Dirolf, who helped catch the errors in this book so the reader wouldn't have to suffer through them.

Much additional appreciation goes to 10gen, the makers of MongoDB, and the wonderful employees who not only provide a great technical product but have also become genuinely close friends over the past few years. In particular, my thanks go out to Jared Rosoff, whose ideas for use cases and design patterns helped inspire (and subsidize!) this book, and to Meghan Gill, for actually putting me back in touch with O'Reilly and getting the process off the ground, as well as providing a wealth of opportunities to attend and speak at various MongoDB conferences.

Thanks go to my children, Matthew and Anna, who've been exceedingly tolerant of a Daddy who loves to play with them in our den but can sometimes only send a hug over Skype.

Finally, and as always, my heartfelt gratitude goes out to my wonderful and beloved wife, Nancy, for her support and confidence in me throughout the years and for inspiring me to many greater things than I could have hoped to achieve alone. I couldn't possibly have done this without you.

## PART I

Design Patterns

## CHAPTER 1

To Embed or Reference

When building a new application, often one of the first things you'll want to do is to design its data model. In relational databases such as MySQL, this step is formalized in the process of normalization, focused on removing redundancy from a set of tables. MongoDB, unlike relational databases, stores its data in structured *documents* rather than the fixed *tables* required in relational databases. For instance, relational tables typically require each row-column intersection to contain a single, scalar value. MongoDB BSON documents allow for more complex structure by supporting arrays of values (where each array itself may be composed of multiple subdocuments).

This chapter explores one of the options that MongoDB's rich document model leaves open to you: the question of whether you should *embed* related objects within one another or *reference* them by ID. Here, you'll learn how to weigh performance, flexibility, and complexity against one another as you make this decision.

Relational Data Modeling and Normalization

Before jumping into MongoDB's approach to the question of embedding documents or linking documents, we'll take a little detour into how you model certain types of relationships in relational (SQL) databases. In relational databases, data modeling typically progresses by modeling your data as a series of *tables*, consisting of *rows* and *columns*, which collectively define the *schema* of your data. Relational database theory has defined a number of ways of putting application data into tables, referred to as *normal forms*. Although a detailed discussion of relational modeling goes beyond the scope of this text, there are two forms that are of particular interest to us here: first normal form and third normal form.

What Is a Normal Form, Anyway?

Schema normalization typically begins by putting your application data into the first normal form (1NF). Although there are specific rules that define exactly what 1NF means, that's a little beyond what we want to cover here. For our purposes, we can consider 1NF data to be any data that's *tabular* (composed of rows and columns), with each row-column intersection ("cell") containing exactly one value. This requirement that each cell contains exactly one value is, as we'll see later, a requirement that MongoDB does not impose, with the potential for some nice performance gains. Back in our relational case, let's consider a phone book application. Your initial data might be of the following form, shown in Table 1-1.

Table 1-1. Phone book v1

id	name	phone_number	zip_code
1	Rick	555-111-1234	30062
2	Mike	555-222-2345	30062
3	Jenny	555-333-3456	01209

This data is actually already in first normal form. Suppose, however, that we wished to allow for multiple phone numbers for each contact, as in Table 1-2.

Table 1-2. Phone book v2

id	name	phone_numbers	zip_code
1	Rick	555-111-1234	30062
2	Mike	555-222-2345;555-212-2322	30062
3	Jenny	555-333-3456;555-334-3411	01209

Now we have a table that's no longer in first normal form. If we were to actually store data in this form in a relational database, we would have to decide whether to store phone_numbers as an unstructured BLOB of text or as separate columns (i.e., phone_number0, phone_number1). Suppose we decided to store phone_numbers as a text column, as shown in Table 1-2. If we needed to implement something like caller ID, finding the name for a given phone number, our SQL query would look something like the following:

```
SELECT name FROM contacts WHERE phone_numbers LIKE '%555-222-2345%';
```

Unfortunately, using a LIKE clause that's not a prefix means that this query requires a full table scan to be satisfied.

Alternatively, we can use multiple columns, one for each phone number, as shown in Table 1-3.

Table 1-3. Phone book v2.1 (multiple columns)

id	name	phone_number0	phone_number1	zip_code
1	Rick	555-111-1234	NULL	30062
2	Mike	555-222-2345	555-212-2322	30062
3	Jenny	555-333-3456	555-334-3411	01209

In this case, our caller ID query becomes quite verbose:

```
SELECT name FROM contacts
    WHERE phone_number0='555-222-2345'
        OR phone_number1='555-222-2345';
```

Updates are also more complicated, particularly deleting a phone number, since we either need to parse the phone_numbers field and rewrite it or find and nullify the matching phone number field. First normal form addresses these issues by breaking up multiple phone numbers into multiple rows, as in Table 1-4.

Table 1-4. Phone book v3

id	name	phone_number	zip_code
1	Rick	555-111-1234	30062
2	Mike	555-222-2345	30062
2	Mike	555-212-2322	30062
2	Jenny	555-333-3456	01209
2	Jenny	555-334-3411	01209

Now we're back to first normal form, but we had to introduce some redundancy into our data model. The problem with redundancy, of course, is that it introduces the possibility of inconsistency, where various copies of the same data have different values. To remove this redundancy, we need to further normalize the data by splitting it into two tables: Table 1-5 and Table 1-6. (And don't worry, we'll be getting back to MongoDB and how it can solve your redundancy problems without normalization really soon now.)

Table 1-5. Phone book v4 (contacts)

contact_id	name	zip_code
1	Rick	30062
2	Mike	30062
3	Jenny	01209

Table 1-6. Phone book v4 (numbers)

contact_id	phone_number
1	555-111-1234
2	555-222-2345
2	555-212-2322
3	555-333-3456
3	555-334-3411

As part of this step, we must identify a *key* column which uniquely identifies each row in the table so that we can create links between the tables. In the data model presented in Table 1-5 and Table 1-6, the `contact_id` forms the key of the *contacts* table, and the (`contact_id`, `phone_number`) pair forms the key of the *numbers* table. In this case, we have a data model that is free of redundancy, allowing us to update a contact's name, zip code, or various phone numbers without having to worry about updating multiple rows. In particular, we no longer need to worry about *inconsistency* in the data model.

So What's the Problem?

As already mentioned, the nice thing about normalization is that it allows for easy updating without any redundancy. Each fact about the application domain can be updated by changing just one value, at one row-column intersection. The problem arises when you try to get the data back *out*. For instance, in our phone book application, we may want to have a form that displays a contact along with *all* of his or her phone numbers. In cases like these, the relational database programmer reaches for a `JOIN`:

```
SELECT name, phone_number
  FROM contacts LEFT JOIN numbers
    ON contacts.contact_id=numbers.contact_id
  WHERE contacts.contact_id=3;
```

The result of this query? A result set like that shown in Table 1-7.

Table 1-7. Result of JOIN query

name	phone_number
Jenny	555-333-3456
Jenny	555-334-3411

Indeed, the database has given us all the data we need to satisfy our screen design. The real problem is in what the database had to do to *create* this result set, particularly if the database is backed by a spinning magnetic disk. To see why, we need to briefly look at some of the physical characteristics of such devices.

Spinning disks have the property that it takes *much* longer to *seek* to a particular location on the disk than it does, once there, to sequentially *read* data from the disk (see

Figure 1-1). For instance, a modern disk might take 5 milliseconds to seek to the place where it can begin reading. Once it is there, however, it can read data at a rate of 40–80 MBs per second. For an application like our phone book, then, assuming a generous 1,024 bytes per row, reading a row off the disk would take between 12 and 25 *microseconds*.

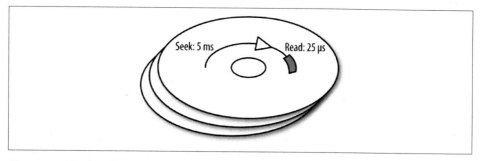

Figure 1-1. Disk seek versus sequential access

The end result of all this math? The seek takes well over 99% of the time spent reading a row. When it comes to disk access, random seeks are the enemy. The reason why this is so important in this context is because JOINs typically require random seeks. Given our normalized data model, a likely plan for our query would be something similar to the following Python code:

```
for number_row in find_by_contact_id(numbers, 3):
    yield (contact_row.name, number_row.number)
```

So there ends up being at least one disk seek for every contact in our database. Of course, we've glossed over how find_by_contact_id works, assuming that *all* it needs to do is a single disk seek. Typically, this is actually accomplished by reading an index on numbers that is keyed by contact_id, potentially resulting in even more disk seeks.

Of course, modern database systems have evolved structures to mitigate some of this, largely by caching frequently used objects (particularly indexes) in RAM. However, even with such optimizations, joining tables is one of the most expensive operations that relational databases do. Additionally, if you end up needing to scale your database to multiple servers, you introduce the problem of generating a *distributed join*, a complex and generally slow operation.

Denormalizing for Performance

The dirty little secret (which isn't really so secret) about relational databases is that once we have gone through the data modeling process to generate our nice *n*th normal form data model, it's often necessary to *denormalize* the model to reduce the number of JOIN operations required for the queries we execute frequently.

In this case, we might just revert to storing the `name` and `contact_id` redundantly in the row. Of course, doing this results in the redundancy we were trying to get away from, and leads to greater application complexity, as we have to make sure to update data in all its redundant locations.

MongoDB: Who Needs Normalization, Anyway?

Into this mix steps MongoDB with the notion that your data doesn't always have to be tabular, basically throwing most of traditional database normalization out, starting with first normal form. In MongoDB, data is stored in *documents*. This means that where the first normal form in relational databases required that each row-column intersection contain exactly *one* value, MongoDB allows you to store an *array* of values if you so desire.

Fortunately for us as application designers, that opens up some new possibilities in schema design. Because MongoDB can natively encode such multivalued properties, we can get many of the performance benefits of a denormalized form without the attendant difficulties in updating redundant data. Unfortunately for us, it also complicates our schema design process. There is no longer a "garden path" of normalized database design to go down, and the go-to answer when faced with general schema design problems in MongoDB is "it depends."

MongoDB Document Format

Before getting into detail about when and why to use MongoDB's array types, let's review just what a MongoDB document is. *Documents* in MongoDB are modeled after the JSON (JavaScript Object Notation) format, but are actually stored in BSON (Binary JSON). Briefly, what this means is that a MongoDB document is a dictionary of key-value pairs, where the value may be one of a number of types:

- Primitive JSON types (e.g., number, string, Boolean)
- Primitive BSON types (e.g., datetime, ObjectId, UUID, regex)
- Arrays of values
- Objects composed of key-value pairs
- Null

In our example phone book application, we might store Jenny's contact information in a document as follows:

```
{
  "_id": 3,
  "name": "Jenny",
  "zip_code": "01209",
```

```
    "numbers": [ "555-333-3456", "555-334-3411" ]
  }
```

As you can see, we're now able to store contact information in the initial Table 1-2 format without going through the process of normalization. Alternatively, we *could* "normalize" our model to remove the array, referencing the contact document by its _id field:

```
// Contact document:
{
  "_id": 3,
  "name": "Jenny",
  "zip_code": "01209"
}

// Number documents:
{ "contact_id": 3, "number": "555-333-3456" }
{ "contact_id": 3, "number": "555-334-3411" }
```

The remainder of this chapter is devoted to helping you decide whether referencing or embedding is the correct solution in various contexts.

Embedding for Locality

One reason you might want to embed your one-to-many relationships is data locality. As discussed earlier, spinning disks are very good at sequential data transfer and very bad at random seeking. And since MongoDB stores documents contiguously on disk, putting all the data you need into one document means that you're never more than one seek away from everything you need.

MongoDB also has a limitation (driven by the desire for easy database partitioning) that there are no JOIN operations available. For instance, if you used referencing in the phone book application, your application might do something like the following:

```
contact_info = db.contacts.find_one({'_id': 3})
number_info = list(db.numbers.find({'contact_id': 3}))
```

If we take this approach, however, we're left with a problem that's actually *worse* than a relational 'JOIN` operation. Not only does the database still have to do multiple seeks to find our data, but we've also introduced additional latency into the lookup since it now takes *two* round-trips to the database to retrieve our data. Thus, if your application frequently accesses contacts' information along with all their phone numbers, you'll almost certainly want to embed the numbers within the contact record.

Embedding for Atomicity and Isolation

Another concern that weighs in favor of embedding is the desire for *atomicity* and *isolation* in writing data. When we update data in our database, we want to ensure that our update either succeeds or fails entirely, never having a "partial success," and that any other database reader never sees an incomplete write operation. Relational databases achieve this by using multistatement *transactions*. For instance, if we want to DELETE Jenny from our normalized database, we might execute code similar to the following:

```
BEGIN TRANSACTION;
DELETE FROM contacts WHERE contact_id=3;
DELETE FROM numbers WHERE contact_id=3;
COMMIT;
```

The problem with using this approach in MongoDB is that MongoDB is designed *without* multidocument transactions. If we tried to delete Jenny from our "normalized" MongoDB schema, we would need to execute the following code:

```
db.contacts.remove({'_id': 3})
db.numbers.remove({'contact_id': 3})
```

Why no transactions?

MongoDB was designed from the ground up to be easy to scale to multiple distributed servers. Two of the biggest problems in distributed database design are distributed join operations and distributed transactions. Both of these operations are complex to implement, and can yield poor performance or even downtime in the event that a server becomes unreachable. By "punting" on these problems and not supporting joins or multidocument transactions at all, MongoDB has been able to implement an automatic sharding solution with much better scaling and performance characteristics than you'd normally be stuck with if you had to take relational joins and transactions into account.

Using this approach, we introduce the possibility that Jenny could be removed from the contacts collection but have her numbers remain in the numbers collection. There's also the possibility that another process reads the database after Jenny's been removed from the contacts collection, but before her numbers have been removed. On the other hand, if we use the embedded schema, we can remove Jenny from our database with a single operation:

```
db.contacts.remove({'_id': 3})
```

One point of interest is that many relational database systems relax the requirement that transactions be completely isolated from one another, introducing various *isolation levels*. Thus, if you can structure your updates to be single-document updates only, you can get the effect of the *serialized* (most conservative) isolation level without any of the performance hits in a relational database system.

Referencing for Flexibility

In many cases, embedding is the approach that will provide the best performance and data consistency guarantees. However, in some cases, a more normalized model works better in MongoDB. One reason you might consider normalizing your data model into multiple collections is the increased flexibility this gives you in performing queries.

For instance, suppose we have a blogging application that contains posts and comments. One approach would be to use an embedded schema:

```
{
  "_id": "First Post",
  "author": "Rick",
  "text": "This is my first post",
  "comments": [
      { "author": "Stuart", "text": "Nice post!" },
      ...
      ]
}
```

Although this schema works well for creating and displaying comments and posts, suppose we wanted to add a feature that allows you to search for all the comments by a particular user. The query (using this embedded schema) would be the following:

```
db.posts.find(
    {'comments.author': 'Stuart'},
    {'comments': 1})
```

The result of this query, then, would be documents of the following form:

```
{ "_id": "First Post",
  "comments": [
      { "author": "Stuart", "text": "Nice post!" },
      { "author": "Mark", "text": "Dislike!" } ] },
{ "_id": "Second Post",
  "comments": [
      { "author": "Danielle", "text": "I am intrigued" },
      { "author": "Stuart", "text": "I would like to subscribe" } ] }
```

The major drawback to this approach is that we get back *much* more data than we actually need. In particular, we can't ask for just Stuart's comments; we have to ask for posts that Stuart has commented on, which includes all the other comments on those posts as well. Further filtering would then be required in our Python code:

```
def get_comments_by(author):
    for post in db.posts.find(
        {'comments.author': author },
        {'comments': 1 }):
        for comment in post['comments']:
            if comment['author'] == author:
                yield post['_id'], comment
```

On the other hand, suppose we decided to use a normalized schema:

```
// db.posts schema
{
  "_id": "First Post",
  "author": "Rick",
  "text": "This is my first post"
}

// db.comments schema
{
  "_id": ObjectId(...),
  "post_id": "First Post",
  "author": "Stuart",
  "text": "Nice post!"
}
```

Our query to retrieve all of Stuart's comments is now quite straightforward:

```
db.comments.find({"author": "Stuart"})
```

In general, if your application's query pattern is well-known and data tends to be accessed in only one way, an embedded approach works well. Alternatively, if your application may query data in many different ways, or you are not able to anticipate the patterns in which data may be queried, a more "normalized" approach may be better. For instance, in our "linked" schema, we're able to sort the comments we're interested in, or restrict the number of comments returned from a query using limit() and skip() operators, whereas in the embedded case, we're stuck retrieving all the comments in the same order they are stored in the post.

Referencing for Potentially High-Arity Relationships

Another factor that may weigh in favor of a more normalized model using document references is when you have one-to-many relationships with very high or unpredictable *arity*. For instance, a popular blog with a large amount of reader engagement may have hundreds or even thousands of comments for a given post. In this case, embedding carries significant penalties with it:

- The larger a document is, the more RAM it uses.
- Growing documents must eventually be copied to larger spaces.
- MongoDB documents have a hard size limit of 16 MB.

The problem with taking up too much RAM is that RAM is usually the most critical resource on a MongoDB server. In particular, a MongoDB database caches frequently accessed documents in RAM, and the larger those documents are, the fewer that will fit. The fewer documents in RAM, the more likely the server is to page fault to retrieve documents, and ultimately page faults lead to random disk I/O.

In the case of our blogging platform, we may only wish to display the first three comments by default when showing a blog entry. Storing all 500 comments along with the entry, then, is simply wasting that RAM in most cases.

The second point, that growing documents need to be copied, has to do with *update* performance. As you append to the embedded comments array, eventually MongoDB is going to need to move the document to an area with more space available. This movement, when it happens, *significantly* slows update performance.

The final point, about the size limit of MongoDB documents, means that if you have a potentially *unbounded* arity in your relationship, it is possible to run out of space entirely, preventing new comments from being posted on an entry. Although this is something to be aware of, you will usually run into problems due to memory pressure and document copying well before you reach the 16 MB size limit.

Many-to-Many Relationships

One final factor that weighs in favor of using document references is the case of many-to-many or M:N relationships. For instance, suppose we have an ecommerce system storing products and categories. Each product may be in multiple categories, and each category may contain multiple products. One approach we could use would be to mimic a relational many-to-many schema and use a "join collection":

```
// db.product schema
{ "_id": "My Product", ... }

// db.category schema
{ "_id": "My Category", ... }

// db.product_category schema
{ "_id": ObjectId(...),
  "product_id": "My Product",
  "category_id": "My Category" }
```

Although this approach gives us a nicely normalized model, our queries end up doing a lot of application-level "joins":

```
def get_product_with_categories(product_id):
    product = db.product.find_one({"_id": product_id})
    category_ids = [
        p_c['category_id']
        for p_c in db.product_category.find(
            { "product_id": product_id }) ]
    categories = db.category.find({
        "_id": { "$in": category_ids } })
    return product, categories
```

Retrieving a category with its products is similarly complex. Alternatively, we can store the objects completely embedded in one another:

```
// db.product schema
{ "_id": "My Product",
  "categories": [
      { "_id": "My Category", ... }
      ...] }
```

```
// db.category schema
{ "_id": "My Category",
  "products": [
    { "_id": "My Product", ... }
    ...] }
```

Our query is now much simpler:

```
def get_product_with_categories(product_id):
    return db.product.find_one({"_id": product_id})
```

Of course, if we want to update a product or a category, we must update it in its own collection as well as every place where it has been embedded into another document:

```
def save_product(product):
    db.product.save(product)
    db.category.update(
        { 'products._id': product['_id'] },
        { '$set': { 'products.*': product } },
        multi=True)
```

For many-to-many joins, a compromise approach is often best, embedding a list of _id values rather than the full document:

```
// db.product schema
{ "_id": "My Product",
  "category_ids": [ "My Category", ... ] }
```

```
// db.category schema
{ "_id": "My Category" }
```

Our query is now a bit more complex, but we no longer need to worry about updating a product everywhere it's included in a category:

```
def get_product_with_categories(product_id):
    product = db.product.find_one({"_id": product_id})
    categories = list(db.category.find({
        '_id': {'$in': product['category_ids']} }))
    return product, categories
```

Conclusion

Schema design in MongoDB tends to be more of an art than a science, and one of the earlier decisions you need to make is whether to *embed* a one-to-many relationship as an array of subdocuments or whether to follow a more relational approach and *reference* documents by their _id value.

The two largest benefits to embedding subdocuments are data locality within a document and the ability of MongoDB to make atomic updates to a document (but not between two documents). Weighing against these benefits is a reduction in flexibility when you embed, as you've "pre-joined" your documents, as well as a potential for problems if you have a high-arity relationship.

Ultimately, the decision depends on the access patterns of your application, and there are fewer hard-and-fast rules in MongoDB than there are in relational databases. Using wisely the flexibility that MongoDB gives you in schema design will help you get the most out of this powerful nonrelational database.

## CHAPTER 2

Polymorphic Schemas

MongoDB is sometimes referred to as a "schemaless" database, meaning that it does not enforce a particular structure on documents in a collection. It is perfectly legal (though of questionable utility) to store every object in your application in the same collection, regardless of its structure. In a well-designed application, however, it is more frequently the case that a collection will contain documents of identical, or closely related, structure. When all the documents in a collection are similarly, but not identically, structured, we call this a *polymorphic schema*.

In this chapter, we'll explore the various reasons for using a polymorphic schema, the types of data models that they can enable, and the methods of such modeling. You'll learn how to use polymorphic schemas to build powerful and flexible data models.

Polymorphic Schemas to Support Object-Oriented Programming

In the world of object-oriented (OO) programming, developers have become accustomed to the ability to have different classes of objects that share data and behavior through *inheritance*. In particular, OO languages allow functions to manipulate *child* classes as though they were their *parent* classes, calling methods that are defined in the parent but may have been overridden with different implementations in the child. This feature of OO languages is referred to as *polymorphism*.

Relational databases, with their focus on tables with a fixed schema, don't support this feature all that well. It would be useful in such cases if our relational database management system (RDBMS) allowed us to define a related set of schemas for a table so that we could store any object in our hierarchy in the same table (and retrieve it using the same mechanism).

For instance, consider a content management system that needs to store wiki pages and photos. Many of the fields stored for wiki pages and photos will be similar, including:

- The title of the object
- Some locator that locates the object in the URL space of the CMS
- Access controls for the object

Some of the fields, of course, will be distinct. The photo doesn't need to have a long markup field containing its text, and the wiki page doesn't need to have a large binary field containing the photo data. In a relational database, there are several options for modeling such an inheritance hierarchy:

- We could create a single table containing a *union* of all the fields that any object in the hierarchy might contain, but this is wasteful of space since no row will populate all its fields.
- We could create a table for each concrete instance (in this case, photo and wiki page), but this introduces redundancy in our schema (anything in common between photos and wiki pages) as well as complicating any type of query where we want to retrieve all content "nodes" (including photos *and* wiki pages).
- We could create a common table for a base content "node" class that we join with an appropriate concrete table. This is referred to as polymorphic inheritance modeling, and removes the redundancy from the concrete-table approach without wasting the space of the single-table approach.

If we assume the polymorphic approach, we might end up with a schema similar to that shown in Table 2-1, Table 2-2, and Table 2-3.

Table 2-1. "Nodes" table

node_id	title	url	type
1	Welcome	/	page
2	About	/about	page
3	Cool Photo	/photo.jpg	photo

Table 2-2. "Pages" table

node_id	text
1	Welcome to my wonderful wiki.
2	This is text that is about the wiki.

Table 2-3. "Photos" table

node_id	content
3	… binary data …

In MongoDB, on the other hand, we can store all of our content node types in the same collection, storing only *relevant* fields in each document:

```
// "Page" document (stored in "nodes" collection")
{
  _id: 1,
  title: "Welcome",
  url: "/",
  type: "page",
  text: "Welcome to my wonderful wiki."
}
...

// "Photo" document (also in "nodes" collection)
{
  _id: 3,
  title: "Cool Photo",
  url: "/photo.jpg",
  type: "photo",
  content: Binary(...)
}
```

If we use such a polymorphic schema in MongoDB, we can use the same collection to perform queries on common fields shared by all content nodes, as well as queries for only a particular node type. For instance, when deciding what to display for a given URL, the CMS needs to look up the node by URL and then perform type-specific formatting to display it. In a relational database, we might execute something like the following:

```
SELECT nodes.node_id, nodes.title, nodes.type,
       pages.text, photos.content
  FROM nodes
    LEFT JOIN pages ON nodes.node_id=pages.node_id
    LEFT JOIN photos ON nodes.node_id=pages.node_id
  WHERE url=:url;
```

Notice in particular that we are performing a three-way join, which will slow down the query substantially. Of course, we could have chosen the single-table model, in which case our query is quite simple:

```
SELECT * FROM nodes WHERE url=:url;
```

In the single-table inheritance model, however, we still retain the drawback of large amounts of wasted space in each row. If we had chosen the concrete-table inheritance model, we would actually have to perform a query for *each type* of content node:

```
SELECT * FROM pages WHERE url=:url;
SELECT * FROM photos WHERE url=:url;
```

In MongoDB, the query is as simple as the single-table model, with the efficiency of the concrete-table model:

```
db.nodes.find_one({url:url})
```

Polymorphic Schemas Enable Schema Evolution

When developing a database-driven application, one concern that programmers must take into account is *schema evolution*. Typically, this is taken care of using a set of *migration* scripts that upgrade the database from one version of a schema to another. Before an application is actually deployed with "live" data, the "migrations" may consist of dropping the database and re-creating it with a new schema. Once your application is live and populated with customer data, however, schema changes require complex migration scripts to change the *format* of data while preserving its *content*.

Relational databases typically support migrations via the ALTER TABLE statement, which allows the developer to add or remove columns from a table. For instance, suppose we wanted to add a short description field to our nodes table from Table 2-1. The SQL for this operation would be similar to the following:

```
ALTER TABLE nodes
    ADD COLUMN short_description varchar(255);
```

The main drawbacks to the ALTER TABLE statement is that it can be time consuming to run on a table with a large number of rows, and may require that your application experience some downtime while the migration executes, since the ALTER TABLE statement needs to hold a lock that your application requires to execute.

In MongoDB, we have the option of doing something similar by updating all documents in a collection to reflect a new field:

```
db.nodes.update(
    {},
    {$set: { short_description: '' } },
    false, // upsert
    true // multi
    );
```

This approach, however, has the same drawbacks as an ALTER TABLE statement: it can be slow, and it can impact the performance of your application negatively.

Another option for MongoDB users is to update your application to account for the absence of the new field. In Python, we might write the following code to handle retrieving both "old style" documents (without a short_description field) as well as "new style" documents (with a short_description field):

```
def get_node_by_url(url):
    node = db.nodes.find_one({'url': url})
    node.setdefault('short_description', '')
    return node
```

Once we have the code in place to handle documents with or without the short_de
scription field, we might choose to gradually migrate the collection in the background,
while our application is running. For instance, we might migrate 100 documents at a
time:

```
def add_short_descriptions():
    node_ids_to_migrate = db.nodes.find(
        {'short_description': {'$exists':False}}).limit(100)
    db.nodes.update(
        { '_id': {'$in': node_ids_to_migrate } },
        { '$set': { 'short_description': '' } },
        multi=True)
```

Once the entire collection is migrated, we can replace our application code to load the
node by URL to omit the default:

```
def get_node_by_url(url):
    node = db.nodes.find_one({'url': url})
    return node
```

Storage (In-)Efficiency of BSON

There is one major drawback to MongoDB's lack of schema enforcement, and that is
storage efficiency. In a RDBMS, since all the column names and types are defined at the
table level, this information does not need to be replicated in each row. MongoDB, by
contrast, *doesn't* know, at the collection level, what fields are present in each document,
nor does it know their types, so this information must be stored on a per-document
basis. In particular, if you are storing small values (integers, datetimes, or short strings)
in your documents and are using long property names, then MongoDB will tend to use
a much larger amount of storage than an RDBMS would for the same data. One approach
to mitigating this in MongoDB is to use short field names in your documents, but this
approach can make it more difficult to inspect the database directly from the shell.

Object-Document Mappers

One approach that can help with storage efficiency *and* with migrations is the use of a
MongoDB object-document mapper (ODM). There are several ODMs available for
Python, including MongoEngine, MongoKit, and Ming. In Ming, for example, you
might create a "Photo" model as follows:

```
class Photo(Document):
    ...
    short_description = Field('sd', str, if_missing='')
    ...
```

Using such a schema, Ming will *lazily* migrate documents as they are loaded from the database, as well as renaming the short_description field (in Python) to the sd property (in BSON).

Polymorphic Schemas Support Semi-Structured Domain Data

In some applications, we may want to store semi-structured domain data. For instance, we may have a product table in a database where products may have various attributes, but not all products have all attributes. One approach to such modeling, of course, is to define all the product classes we're interested in storing and use the object-oriented mapping approach just described. There are, however, some pitfalls to avoid when this approach meets data in the real business world:

- Product hierarchies may change frequently as items are reclassified
- Many products, even within the same class, may have incomplete data

For instance, suppose we are storing a database of disk drives. Although all drives in our inventory specify capacity, some may also specify the cache size, while others omit it. In this case, we can use a generic properties subdocument containing the variable fields:

```
{
  _id: ObjectId(...),
  price: 499.99,
  title: 'Big and Fast Disk Drive',
  gb_capacity: 1000,
  properties: {
    'Seek Time': '5ms',
    'Rotational Speed': '15k RPM',
    'Transfer Rate': '...'
    ... }
}
```

The drawback to storing semi-structured data in this way is that it's difficult to perform queries and indexing on fields that you wish your application to be ignorant of. Another approach you might use is to keep an array of property-value pairs:

```
{
  _id: ObjectId(...),
  price: 499.99,
  title: 'Big and Fast Disk Drive',
  gb_capacity: 1000,
  properties: [
    ['Seek Time', '5ms' ],
    ['Rotational Speed', '15k RPM'],
    ['Transfer Rate', '...'],
```

```
    ... ]
  }
```

If we use the array of properties approach, we can instruct MongoDB to index the properties field with the following command:

```
db.products.ensure_index('properties')
```

Once this field is indexed, our queries simply specify the property-value pairs we're interested in:

```
db.products.find({'properties': [ 'Seek Time': '5ms' ]})
```

Doing the equivalent operation in a relational database requires more cumbersome approaches, such as entity-attribute-value schemas, covered in more detail in "Entity attribute values" (page 77).

Conclusion

The flexibility that MongoDB offers by not enforcing a particular schema for all documents in a collection provides several benefits to the application programmer over an RDBMS solution:

- Better mapping of object-oriented inheritance and polymorphism
- Simpler migrations between schemas with less application downtime
- Better support for semi-structured domain data

Effectively using MongoDB requires recognizing when a polymorphic schema may benefit your application and not over-normalizing your schema by replicating the same data layout you might use for a relational database system.

## CHAPTER 3

Mimicking Transactional Behavior

Relational database schemas often rely on the existence of atomic multistatement transactions to ensure data consistency: either all of the statements in a group succeed, or all of the statements fail, moving the database from one self-consistent state to another. When trying to scale relational databases over multiple physical servers, however, transactions must use a two-phase commit protocol, which significantly slows down transactions that may span multiple servers. MongoDB, in not allowing multidocument atomic transactions, effectively side-steps this problem and substitutes another one: how to maintain consistency in the *absence* of transactions.

In this chapter, we'll explore how MongoDB's document model and its atomic update operations enable an approach that maintains consistency where a relational database would use a transaction. We'll also look at how we can use an approach known as *compensation* to mimic the transactional behavior of relational databases.

The Relational Approach to Consistency

One of the goals of relational database normalization is the ability to make atomic changes to a single row, which maintains the domain-level consistency of your data model. Although normalization goes a long way toward such consistency enforcement, there are some types of consistency requirements that are difficult or impossible to express in a single SQL statement:

- Deleting a row in a one-to-many relationship should also delete the many rows joined to it. For instance, deleting an order from the system should delete its subordinate rows.

- Adjusting the quantity of a line item on an order should update the order total cost (assuming that cost is stored in the order row itself).

- In a bank account transfer, the debit from the sending account and the credit into the receiving account should be an atomic operation where both succeed or both fail. Additionally, other simultaneous transactions should not see the data in an incomplete state where either the debit or credit has not yet completed.

To address situations such as these, relational databases use atomic multistatement transactions, where a group of updates to a database either all succeed (via COMMIT) or all fail (via ROLLBACK). The drawback to multistatement transactions is that they can be quite slow if you are using a distributed database. However, it is possible to maintain consistency across multiple servers in a distributed database using a two-phase commit protocol, summarized as follows:

1. Each server prepares to execute the transaction. In this stage, all the updates are computed and guaranteed not to cause consistency violations within the server.

2. Once all servers have executed the "prepare" step, each server then applies the updates that are part of the transaction.

The drawback to a two-phase commit is that it can significantly slow down your application. Since each server guarantees that the transaction can be completed at the end of the prepare step, the server will typically maintain a set of locks on data to be modified. These locks must then be held until all the *other* servers have completed *their* prepare step, which may be a lengthy process.

MongoDB, designed from the beginning with an eye toward distributed operation, "solves" this problem by giving up on the idea of multidocument transactions. In MongoDB, each update to a document stands alone.

Compound Documents

MongoDB's document model and its update operators combine to enable operations that would require transactions in relational databases. For example, consider deleting an order from a database where each order contains multiple line items. In a relational database, we could use a transaction to ensure that the order "cleans up after itself":

```
BEGIN TRANSACTION;
DELETE FROM orders WHERE id='11223';
DELETE FROM order_items WHERE order_id='11223';
COMMIT;
```

Since this is such a common use case, many relational database systems provide cascading constraints in the table-creation logic that do this automatically. For instance, we may have designed our tables using the following SQL:

```
CREATE TABLE `orders` (
    `id` CHAR(5) NOT NULL,
    ...
```

```
    PRIMARY KEY(`id`))

CREATE TABLE `order_items` (
    `order_id` CHAR(5) NOT NULL,
    `sku` CHAR(8) NOT NULL,
    ...
    PRIMARY KEY(`order_id`, `sku`),
    FOREIGN KEY(`order_id`) REFERENCES orders.id
        ON DELETE CASCADE)
```

In this case, we could execute a simpler SQL statement:

```
DELETE FROM orders WHERE id='11223';
```

However, despite the fact that we're not explicitly calling BEGIN and COMMIT, the database system is still doing the work of a full, multitable transaction.

A developer new to MongoDB may approach an order management system by designing a relational-style schema:

```
// "orders" document
{
  _id: '11223',
  ...
}

// "order_items" document
{
  _id: ObjectId(...),
  order_id: '11223',
  sku: '...',
  ...
}
```

Deleting such an order, however, presents a problem. One approach is to use two non-atomic updates:

```
db.orders.remove({'_id': '1123'})
db.order_items.remove({'order_id': '11223'})
```

Of course, this can leave dangling order_items documents around if an exception occurs between the remove calls, and other processes can end up seeing orphaned order_items documents if they happen to query that collection between our operations. Alternatively, we could reverse the order:

```
db.order_items.remove({'order_id': '11223'})
db.orders.remove({'_id': '1123'})
```

Although this guarantees that we won't have "garbage" items in our database, it also introduces the problem of having partially deleted orders, where some or all of the line items are deleted but the order itself remains. A better approach is to simply embed the order items within the order document itself:

```
// "orders" document
{
  _id: '11223',
  ...
  items: [
    { sku: '...', ... },
    { sku: '...', ... },
    ...
  ]
}
```

Deleting the order, then, is as simple as the single statement:

```
db.orders.remove({'_id': '1123'})
```

Using Complex Updates

Although using document embedding in your MongoDB schema makes some "trans-actional" problems in relational databases easier to handle, there are other cases where we need something more. For instance, consider our order management system again. Suppose we wish to store the order total price as well as each line item's price so that we can easily display the order total without computing it each time. A document might look like the following:

```
// "orders" document
{
  _id: '11223',
  total: 500.94,
  ...
  items: [
    { sku: '123', price: 55.11, qty: 2 },
    { sku: '...', ... },
    ...
  ]
}
```

Now suppose we want to update the quantity of item 123 to 3. A naive approach might be to read the document from the database, update it in-memory, and then save it back. Unfortunately, this approach introduces race conditions between the loading of the order and saving it back. What we need is a way to atomically update the document *without* doing it in client application code. We can use MongoDB's atomic update oper-ators to perform the same operation in a single step. We *might* do so with the following code:

```
def increase_qty(order_id, sku, price, qty):
    total_update = price * qty
    while True:
        db.orders.update(
            { '_id': order_id, 'items.sku': sku },
            { '$inc': {
```

```
                        'total': total_update,
                        'items.$.qty': qty } })
```

In this case, we still have a risk that another operation *removed* the line item we are interested in updating (perhaps in another browser window). To account for this case, we must detect whether our update actually succeeds by checking its return value. If the update failed, someone must have removed that line item and we must try to $push it onto the array with its new quantity:

```
def increase_qty(order_id, sku, price, qty):
    total_update = price * qty
    while True:
        result = db.orders.update(
            { '_id': order_id, 'items.sku': sku },
            { '$inc': {
                'total': total_update,
                'items.$.qty': qty } })
        if result['updatedExisting']: break
        result = db.orders.update(
            { '_id': order_id, 'items.sku': { '$ne': sku } },
            { '$inc': { 'total': 110.22 },
              '$push': { 'items': { 'sku': sku,
                                    'qty': qty,
                                    'price': price } } })
        if result['updatedExisting']: break
```

Optimistic Update with Compensation

There are some cases where it's just not possible to do your operation with a single update() statement in MongoDB. For instance, consider the account transfer problem where we must debit one account and credit another. In these cases, we are stuck making multiple updates, but we must ensure that our database is eventually consistent by examining all the places where we could have an error. A naive approach would simply store the account balance in each document and update them separately. Our documents would be quite simple:

```
{ _id: 1, balance: 100 }
{ _id: 2, balance: 0 }
```

The code to update them is likewise simple:

```
def transfer(amt, source, destination):
    result = db.accounts.update(
        { '_id': source, 'balance': { '$gte': amt } },
        { '$inc': { 'balance': -amt } })
    if not result['updatedExisting']:
        raise InsufficientFundsError(source)
    db.accounts.update(
        { '_id': destination },
        { '$inc': { 'balance': amt } } )
```

The problem with this approach is that, if an exception occurs between the source account being debited and the destination account being credited, the funds are lost.

 You should be exceedingly careful if you find yourself designing an application-level, two-phase commit protocol. It's easy to miss a particular failure scenario, and there are many opportunities to miss a race condition and introduce inconsistency into your data, by a small oversight in design or a bug in implementation. As a rule of thumb, whenever it's possible to structure your schema such that all your atomic updates occur *within* a document boundary, you should do so, but it's nice to know you can still fall back to two-phase commit if you absolutely have to.

A better approach to this problem is to emulate transactions in the data model. Our basic approach here will be to create a "transaction" collection containing documents that store the state of all outstanding transfers:

- Any transaction in the "new" state may be rolled back if it times out.
- Any transaction in the "committed" state will always (eventually) be retired.
- Any transaction in the "rollback" state will always (eventually) be reversed.

Our transaction collection contains documents of the following format:

```
{
    _id: ObjectId(...),
    state: 'new',
    ts: ISODateTime(...),
    amt: 55.22,
    src: 1,
    dst: 2
}
```

Our account schema also changes just a bit to store the pending transaction IDs along with each account:

```
{ _id: 1, balance: 100, txns: [] }
{ _id: 2, balance: 0, txns: [] }
```

The top-level transfer function transfers an amount from one account to another as before, but we have added a maximum amount of time allowable for the transaction to complete. If a transaction takes longer, it will eventually be rolled back by a periodic process:

```
def transfer(amt, source, destination, max_txn_time):
    txn = prepare_transfer(amt, source, destination)
    commit_transfer(txn, max_txn_time)
```

Note that in the preceding code we now have a two-phase commit model of our transfer: first the accounts are prepared, then the transaction is committed. The code to prepare the transfer is as follows:

```python
def prepare_transfer(amt, source, destination):
    # Create a transaction object
    now = datetime.utcnow()
    txnid = ObjectId()
    txn = {
        '_id': txnid,
        'state': 'new',
        'ts': datetime.utcnow(),
        'amt': amt,
        'src': source,
        'dst': destination }
    db.transactions.insert(txn)

    # "Prepare" the accounts
    result = db.accounts.update(
        { '_id': source, 'balance': { '$gte': amt } },
        { '$inc': { 'balance': -amt },
          '$push': { 'txns': txn['_id'] } })
    if not result['updatedExisting']:
        db.transaction.remove({'_id': txnid})
        raise InsufficientFundsError(source)
    db.accounts.update(
        { '_id': dest },
        { '$inc': { 'balance': amt },
          '$push': { 'txns': txn['_id'] } })
    return txn
```

There are two key insights applied here:

- The source and destination accounts store a list of pending transactions. This allows us to track, in the account document, whether a particular transaction ID is pending.

- The transaction itself must complete during a certain time window. If it does not, a periodic process will roll outstanding transactions back or commit them based on the last state of the transaction. This handles cases where the application or database crashes in the middle of a transaction.

Here's our function to actually commit the transfer:

```python
def commit_transfer(txn, max_txn_time):
    # Mark the transaction as committed
    now = datetime.utcnow()
    cutoff = now - max_txn_time
    result = db.transaction.update(
        { '_id': txnid, 'state': 'new', 'ts': { '$gt': cutoff } },
        { '$set': { 'state': 'commit' } })
    if not result['updatedExisting']:
        raise TransactionError(txn['_id'])
```

```
    else:
        retire_transaction(txn['_id'])
```

The main purpose of this function is to perform the atomic update of transaction state from new to commit. If this update succeeds, the transaction will eventually be retired, even if a crash occurs immediately after the update. To actually retire the transaction, then, we use the following function:

```
def retire_transaction(txn_id):
    db.accounts.update(
            { '_id': txn['src'], 'txns._id': txn_id },
            { '$pull': { 'txns': txn_id } })
    db.accounts.update(
            { '_id': txn['dst'], 'txns._id': txn['_id'] },
            { '$pull': { 'txns': txn_id } })
    db.transaction.remove({'_id': txn_id})
```

Note that the retire_transaction is *idempotent*: it can be called any number of times with the same txn_id with the same effect as calling it once. This means that if we have a crash at any point before removing the transaction object, a subsequent cleanup process can still retire the transaction by simply calling retire_transaction again.

We now need to take care of transactions that have timed out, or where the commit or rollback process has crashed in a periodic cleanup task:

```
def cleanup_transactions(txn, max_txn_time):
    # Find & commit partially-committed transactions
    for txn in db.transaction.find({ 'state': 'commit' }, {'_id': 1}):
        retire_transaction(txn['_id'])

    # Move expired transactions to 'rollback' status:
    cutoff = now - max_txn_time
    db.transaction.update(
            { '_id': txnid, 'state': 'new', 'ts': { '$lt': cutoff } },
            { '$set': { 'state': 'rollback' } })
    # Actually rollback transactions
    for txn in db.transaction.find({ 'state': 'rollback' }):
        rollback_transfer()
```

Finally, in the case where we want to roll back a transfer, we must update the transaction object and *undo* the effects of the transfer:

```
def rollback_transfer(txn):
    db.accounts.update(
            { '_id': txn['src'], 'txns._id': txn['_id'] },
            { '$inc': { 'balance': txn['amt'] },
              '$pull': { 'txns': { '_id': txn['_id'] } } })
    db.accounts.update(
            { '_id': txn['dst'], 'txns._id': txn['_id'] },
            { '$inc': { 'balance': -txn['amt'] },
              '$pull': { 'txns': { '_id': txn['_id'] } } })
    db.transaction.remove({'_id': txn['_id']})
```

Note in particular that the preceding code will only undo a transaction in an account if the transaction is still stored in that account's `txns` array. This makes the rollback of the transaction idempotent just like retiring a transaction via a commit.

Conclusion

The constraints of a toolset help to define patterns for solving problems. In the case of MongoDB, one of those constraints is the lack of atomic multidocument update operations. The patterns we use in MongoDB to mitigate the lack of atomic multidocument update operations include document embedding and complex updates for basic operations, with optimistic update with compensation available for when we really need a two-phase commit protocol. When designing your application to use MongoDB, more than in relational databases, you must keep in mind which updates you need to be atomic and design your schema appropriately.

PART II
Use Cases

## CHAPTER 4

Operational Intelligence

The first use cases we'll explore lie in the realm of *operational intelligence*, the techniques of converting transactional data to actionable information in a business setting. Of course, the starting point for any of these techniques is getting the raw transactional data *into* your data store. Our first use case, "Storing Log Data" (page 37), deals with this part of the puzzle.

Once you have the data, of course, the first priority is to generate actionable reports on that data, ideally in real time with the data import itself. We address the generation of these reports in real time in "Pre-Aggregated Reports" (page 52).

Finally, we'll explore the use of more traditional batch aggregation in "Hierarchical Aggregation" (page 63) to see how MongoDB can be used to generate reports at multiple layers of your analytics hierarchy.

Storing Log Data

The starting point for any analytics system is the raw "transactional" data. To give a feel for this type of problem, we'll examine the particular use case of storing event data in MongoDB that would traditionally be stored in plain-text logfiles. Although plain-text logs are accessible and human-readable, they are difficult to use, reference, and analyze, frequently being stored on a server's local filesystem in an area that is generally inaccessible to the business analysts who need these data.

Solution Overview

The solution described here assumes that each server generating events can access the MongoDB instance and has read/write access to some database on that instance. Furthermore, we assume that the query rate for logging data is significantly lower than the insert rate for log data.

This case assumes that you're using a standard uncapped collection for this event data, unless otherwise noted. See "Capped collections" (page 51) for another approach to aging out old data.

Schema Design

The schema for storing log data in MongoDB depends on the format of the event data that you're storing. For a simple example, you might consider standard request logs in the combined format from the Apache HTTP Server. A line from these logs may resemble the following:

```
127.0.0.1 - frank [10/Oct/2000:13:55:36 -0700] "GET /apache_pb.gif HTTP/1.0" ...
```

The simplest approach to storing the log data would be putting the exact text of the log record into a document:

```
{
  _id: ObjectId(...),
  line: '127.0.0.1 - frank [10/Oct/2000:13:55:36 -0700] "GET /apache_pb.gif ...
}
```

Although this solution does capture all data in a format that MongoDB can use, the data is neither particularly useful nor efficient. For example, if you need to find events on the same page, you would need to use a regular expression query, which would require a full scan of the collection. A better approach is to extract the relevant information from the log data into individual fields in a MongoDB *document*.

When designing the structure of that document, it's important to pay attention to the data types available for use in BSON, the MongoDB document format. Choosing your data types wisely can have a significant impact on the performance and capability of the logging system. For instance, consider the date field. In the previous example, [10/Oct/2000:13:55:36 -0700] is 28 bytes long. If you store this with the UTC timestamp BSON type, you can convey the same information in only 8 bytes.

Additionally, using proper types for your data also increases query flexibility. If you store date as a timestamp, you can make date range queries, whereas it's very difficult to compare two *strings* that represent dates. The same issue holds for numeric fields; storing numbers as strings requires more space and is more difficult to query.

Consider the following document that captures all data from the log entry:

```
{
    _id: ObjectId(...),
    host: "127.0.0.1",
    logname: null,
    user: 'frank',
    time: ISODate("2000-10-10T20:55:36Z"),
    request: "GET /apache_pb.gif HTTP/1.0",
```

```
        status: 200,
        response_size: 2326,
        referrer: "[http://www.example.com/start.html](http://www.example.com/...",
        user_agent: "Mozilla/4.08 [en] (Win98; I ;Nav)"
}
```

The is better, but it's quite a large document. When extracting data from logs and designing a schema, you should also consider what information you can omit from your
log tracking system. In most cases, there's no need to track *all* data from an event log.
To continue this example, here the most crucial information may be the host, time, path,
user agent, and referrer, as in the following example document:

```
{
        _id: ObjectId(...),
        host: "127.0.0.1",
        time:  ISODate("2000-10-10T20:55:36Z"),
        path: "/apache_pb.gif",
        referer: "[http://www.example.com/start.html](http://www.example.com/...",
        user_agent: "Mozilla/4.08 [en] (Win98; I ;Nav)"
}
```

Depending on your storage and memory requirements, you might even consider omit-
ting explicit time fields, since the BSON `ObjectId` implicitly embeds its own creation
time:

```
{
        _id: ObjectId('...'),
        host: "127.0.0.1",
        path: "/apache_pb.gif",
        referer: "[http://www.example.com/start.html](http://www.example.com/...",
        user_agent: "Mozilla/4.08 [en] (Win98; I ;Nav)"
}
```

Operations

In this section, we'll describe the various operations you'll need to perform on the logging system, paying particular attention to the appropriate use of indexes and
MongoDB-specific features.

Inserting a log record

The primary performance concerns for event-logging systems are:

- How many inserts per second it can support, which limits the event throughput
- How the system will manage the growth of event data, particularly in the case of a
  growth in insert activity

In designing our system, we'll primarily focus on optimizing insertion speed, while still
addressing how we manage event data growth. One decision that MongoDB allows you

to make when performing updates (such as event data insertion) is whether you want to trade off data safety guarantees for increased insertion speed. This section will explore the various options we can tweak depending on our tolerance for event data loss.

Write concern

MongoDB has a configurable *write concern*. This capability allows you to balance the importance of guaranteeing that all writes are fully recorded in the database with the speed of the insert.

For example, if you issue writes to MongoDB and do not require that the database issue any response, the write operations will return *very* fast (since the application needs to wait for a response from the database) but you cannot be certain that all writes succeeded. Conversely, if you require that MongoDB acknowledge every write operation, the database will not return as quickly but you can be certain that every item will be present in the database.

The proper write concern is often an application-specific decision, and depends on the reporting requirements and uses of your analytics application.

In the examples in this section, we will assume that the following code (or something similar) has set up an event from the Apache Log. In a real system, of course, we would need code to actually parse the log and create the Python `dict` shown here:

```
>>> import bson
>>> import pymongo
>>> from datetime import datetime
>>> conn = pymongo.Connection()
>>> db = conn.event_db
>>> event = {
...     _id: bson.ObjectId(),
...     host: "127.0.0.1",
...     time:  datetime(2000,10,10,20,55,36),
...     path: "/apache_pb.gif",
...     referer: "[http://www.example.com/start.html](http://www.example.com/...",
...     user_agent: "Mozilla/4.08 [en] (Win98; I ;Nav)"
...}
```

The following command will insert the `event` object into the `events` collection:

```
>>> db.events.insert(event, w=0)
```

By setting w=0, you do not require that MongoDB acknowledge receipt of the insert. Although this is the fastest option available to us, it also carries with it the risk that you might lose a large number of events before you notice.

If you want to ensure that MongoDB acknowledges inserts, you can omit the `w=0` argument, or pass `w=1` (the default) as follows:

```
>>> db.events.insert(event)
>>> # Alternatively, you can do this
>>> db.events.insert(event, w=1)
```

MongoDB also supports a more stringent level of write concern, if you have a lower tolerance for data loss. MongoDB uses an on-disk journal file to persist data before writing the updates back to the "regular" data files.

Since journal writes are significantly slower than in-memory updates (which are, in turn, much slower than "regular" data file updates), MongoDB batches up journal writes into "group commits" that occur every 100 ms unless overridden in your server settings. What this means for the application developer is that, on average, any individual writes with `j=True` will take around 50 ms to complete, which is generally even more time than it would take to replicate the data to another server. If you want to ensure that MongoDB not only *acknowledges* receipt of a write operation but also commits the write operation to the on-disk journal before returning successfully to the application, you can use the `j=True` option:

```
>>> db.events.insert(event, j=True)
```

It's important to note that the journal does *not* protect against any failure in which the disk itself might fail, since in that case the journal file itself can be corrupted. Replication, however, *does* protect against single-server failures, and is the recommended way to achieve real durability.

 `j=True` requires acknowledgment from the server, so `w=1` is implied unless you explicitly set `w=N` with N greater than 1.

You can require that MongoDB replicate the data to multiple secondary replica set members before returning:

```
>>> db.events.insert(event, w=2)
```

This will force your application to acknowledge that the data has replicated to two members of the replica set. You can combine options as well:

```
>>> db.events.insert(event, j=True, w=2)
```

In this case, your application will wait for a successful journal commit *and* a replication acknowledgment. This is the safest option presented in this section, but it is the slowest. There is always a trade-off between safety and speed.

Bulk inserts

If possible, you should use bulk inserts to insert event data. All write concern options apply to bulk inserts, but you can pass multiple events to the insert() method at once. Batch inserts allow MongoDB to distribute the performance penalty incurred by more stringent write concern across a group of inserts.

If you're doing a bulk insert and *do* get an error (either a network interruption or a unique key violation), your application will need to handle the possibility of a partial bulk insert. If your particular use case doesn't care about missing a few inserts, you can add the continue_on_error=True argument to insert, in which case the insert will insert as many documents as possible, and report an error on the *last* insert that failed.

If you use continue_on_error=True and *multiple* inserts in your batch fail, your application will only receive information on the *last* insert to fail. The take-away? You can sometimes amortize the overhead of safer writes by using bulk inserts, but this technique brings with it another set of concerns as well.

Finding all events for a particular page

The value in maintaining a collection of event data derives from being able to query that data to answer specific questions. You may have a number of simple queries that you may use to analyze these data.

As an example, you may want to return all of the events associated with a specific value of a field. Extending the Apache access log example, a common case would be to query for all events with a specific value in the path field. This section contains a pattern for returning data and optimizing this operation.

In this case, you'd use a query that resembles the following to return all documents with the /apache_pb.gif value in the path field:

```
>>> q_events = db.events.find({'path': '/apache_pb.gif'})
```

Of course, if you want this query to perform well, you'll need to add an index on the path field:

```
>>> db.events.ensure_index('path')
```

Aside: managing index size

One thing you should keep in mind when you're creating indexes is the size they take up in RAM. When an index is accessed randomly, as in the case here with our index on path, the entire index needs to be resident in RAM. In this particular case, the total number of distinct paths is typically small in relation to the number of documents, which will limit the space that the index requires.

To actually see the size of an index, you can use the `collstats` database command:

```
>>> db.command('collstats', 'events')['indexSizes']
```

There is actually another type of index that doesn't take up much RAM, and that's a *right-aligned* index. *Right-aligned* refers to the access pattern of a regular index, not a special MongoDB index type: in this case, most of the queries that use the index focus on the largest (or smallest) values in the index, so most of the index is never actually used. This is often the case with time-oriented data, where you tend to query documents from the recent past. In this case, only a very thin "sliver" of the index is ever resident in RAM at a particular time, so index size is of much less concern.

Finding all the events for a particular date

Another operation we might wish to do is to query the event log for all events that happened on a particular date, perhaps as part of a security audit of suspicious activity. In this case, we'll use a range query:

```
>>> q_events = db.events.find('time':
...     { '$gte':datetime(2000,10,10),'$lt':datetime(2000,10,11)})
```

This query selects documents from the `events` collection where the value of the `time` field represents a date that is on or after (i.e., `$gte`) `2000-10-10` but before (i.e., `$lt`) `2000-10-11`. Here, an index on the `time` field would optimize performance:

```
>>> db.events.ensure_index('time')
```

Note that this is a right-aligned index so long as our queries tend to focus on the recent history.

Finding all events for a particular host/date

Expanding on our "security audit" example, suppose we isolated the incident to a particular server and wanted to look at the activity for only a single server on a particular date. In this case, we'd use a query that resembles the following:

```
>>> q_events = db.events.find({
...     'host': '127.0.0.1',
...     'time': {'$gte':datetime(2000,10,10),'$lt':datetime(2000,10,11)}
... })
```

The indexes you use may have significant implications for the performance of these kinds of queries. For instance, you *can* create a compound index on the time-host field pair (noting that order matters), using the following command:

```
>>> db.events.ensure_index([('time', 1), ('host', 1)])
```

To analyze the performance for the above query using this index, MongoDB provides the `explain()` method. In Python for instance, we can execute `q_events.explain()` in a console. This will return something that resembles:

```
{ ..
  u'cursor': u'BtreeCursor time_1_host_1',
  u'indexBounds': {u'host': [[u'127.0.0.1', u'127.0.0.1']],
  u'time': [
      [ datetime.datetime(2000, 10, 10, 0, 0),
        datetime.datetime(2000, 10, 11, 0, 0)]]
  },
  ...
  u'millis': 4,
  u'n': 11,
  u'nscanned': 1296,
  u'nscannedObjects': 11,
  ... }
```

This query had to scan 1,296 items from the index to return 11 objects in 4 milliseconds. Conversely, you can test a different compound index with the host field first, followed by the time field. Create this index using the following operation:

```
>>> db.events.ensure_index([('host', 1), ('time', 1)])
```

Now, explain() tells us the following:

```
{ ...
  u'cursor': u'BtreeCursor host_1_time_1',
  u'indexBounds': {u'host': [[u'127.0.0.1', u'127.0.0.1']],
  u'time': [[datetime.datetime(2000, 10, 10, 0, 0),
      datetime.datetime(2000, 10, 11, 0, 0)]]},
  ...
  u'millis': 0,
  u'n': 11,
  ...
  u'nscanned': 11,
  u'nscannedObjects': 11,
  ...
}
```

Here, the query had to scan 11 items from the index before returning 11 objects in less than a millisecond. Although the index order has an impact on query performance, remember that index scans are *much* faster than collection scans, and depending on your other queries, it may make more sense to use the { time: 1, host: 1 } index depending on usage profile.

Rules of index design

MongoDB indexes are stored in a data structure known as a B-tree. The details are beyond our scope here, but what you need to understand as a MongoDB *user* is that each index is stored in sorted order on all the fields in the index. For an index to be maximally efficient, the key should look just like the queries that use the index. Ideally, MongoDB should be able to traverse the index to the first document that the query returns and *sequentially walk* the index to find the rest.

Because of this sorted B-tree structure, then, the following rules will lead to efficient indexes:

- Any fields that will be queried *by equality* should occur first in the index definition.
- Fields used to sort should occur next in the index definition. If multiple fields are being sorted (such as (last_name, first_name), then they should occur in the same order in the index definition.
- Fields that are queried by range should occur *last* in the index definition.

This leads to some unfortunate circumstances where our index cannot be used optimally:

- Whenever we have a range query on two or more properties, they cannot both be used effectively in the index.
- Whenever we have a range query combined with a sort on a different property, the index is somewhat less efficient than when doing a range and sort on the same property set.

In such cases, the best approach is to test with representative data, making liberal use of explain(). If you discover that the MongoDB query optimizer is making a bad choice of index (perhaps choosing to reduce the number of entries scanned at the expense of doing a large in-memory sort, for instance), you can also use the hint() method to tell it which index to use.

Counting requests by day and page

Finding requests is all well and good, but more frequently we need to *count* requests, or perform some other aggregate operation on them during analysis. Here, we'll describe how you can use MongoDB's *aggregation framework*, introduced in version 2.1, to select, process, and aggregate results from a large number of documents for powerful ad hoc queries. In this case, we'll count the number of requests per resource (i.e., page) per day in the last month.

To use the aggregation framework, we need to set up a *pipeline* of operations. In this case, our pipeline looks like Figure 4-1 and is implemented by the database command shown here:

```
>>> result = db.command('aggregate', 'events', pipeline=[
...         { '$match': {    ❶
...             'time': {
...                 '$gte': datetime(2000,10,1),
...                 '$lt':  datetime(2000,11,1) } } },
...         { '$project': {    ❷
...             'path': 1,
...             'date': {
```

```
...                          'y': { '$year': '$time' },
...                          'm': { '$month': '$time' },
...                          'd': { '$dayOfMonth': '$time' } } } },
...          { '$group': {  ❸
...                '_id': {
...                     'p':'$path',
...                     'y': '$date.y',
...                     'm': '$date.m',
...                     'd': '$date.d' },
...                'hits': { '$sum': 1 } } },
...          ])
```

This command aggregates documents from the events collection with a pipeline that:

❶ Uses the $match operation to limit the documents that the aggregation framework must process. $match is similar to a find() query. This operation selects all documents where the value of the time field represents a date that is on or after (i.e., $gte) 2000-10-10 but before (i.e., $lt) 2000-10-11.

❷ Uses the $project operator to limit the data that continues through the pipeline. This operator:

- Selects the path field.
- Creates a y field to hold the year, computed from the time field in the original documents.
- Creates an m field to hold the month, computed from the time field in the original documents.
- Creates a d field to hold the day, computed from the time field in the original documents.

❸ Uses the $group operator to create new computed documents. This step will create a single new document for each unique path/date combination. The documents take the following form:

- The _id field holds a subdocument with the content's path field from the original documents in the p field, with the date fields from the $project as the remaining fields.
- The hits field uses the $sum statement to increment a counter for every document in the group. In the aggregation output, this field holds the total number of documents at the beginning of the aggregation pipeline with this unique date and path.

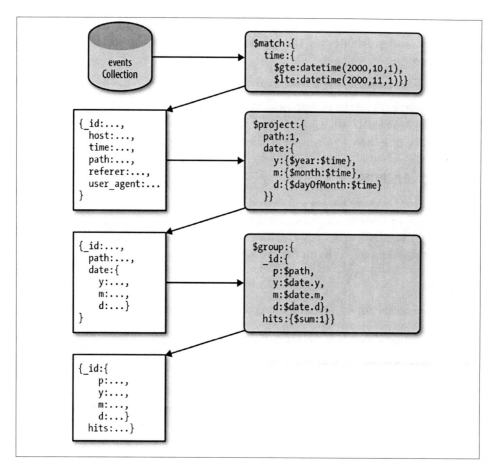

Figure 4-1. Aggregation pipeline

In sharded environments, the performance of aggregation operations depends on the shard key. Ideally, all the items in a particular $group operation will reside on the same server.

Although this distribution of documents would occur if you chose the time field as the shard key, a field like path also has this property and is a typical choice for sharding. See "Sharding Concerns" (page 48) for additional recommendations concerning sharding.

SQL equivalents

To translate statements from the aggregation framework to SQL, you can consider the $match equivalent to WHERE, $project to SELECT, and $group to GROUP BY.

In order to optimize the aggregation operation, you must ensure that the initial `$match` query has an index. In this case, the command would be simple, and it's an index we already have:

```
>>> db.events.ensure_index('time')
```

If you have already created a compound index on the `time` and `host` (i.e., `{ time: 1, host, 1 }`,) MongoDB will use this index for range queries on just the `time` field. In situations like this, there's no benefit to creating an additional index for just `time`.

Sharding Concerns

Eventually, your system's events will exceed the capacity of a single event logging database instance. In these situations you will want to use a *shard cluster*, which takes advantage of MongoDB's automatic sharding functionality. In this section, we introduce the unique sharding concerns for the event logging use case.

Limitations

In a sharded environment, the limitations on the maximum insertion rate are:

- The number of shards in the cluster
- The shard key you choose

Because MongoDB distributes data using *chunks* based on ranges of the *shard key*, the choice of shard key can control how MongoDB distributes data and the resulting systems' capacity for writes and queries.

Ideally, your shard key should have two characteristics:

- Insertions are *balanced* between shards
- Most queries can be *routed* to a subset of the shards to be satisfied

Here are some initially appealing options for shard keys, which on closer examination, fail to meet at least one of these criteria:

Timestamps
> Shard keys based on the timestamp or the insertion time (i.e., the `ObjectId`) end up all going in the "high" chunk, and therefore to a single shard. The inserts are not *balanced*.

Hashes
> If the shard key is random, as with a hash, then all queries must be *broadcast* to all shards. The queries are not *routeable*.

We'll now examine these options in more detail.

Option 1: Shard by time

Although using the timestamp, or the `ObjectId` in the `_id` field, would distribute your data evenly among shards, these keys lead to two problems:

- All inserts always flow to the same shard, which means that your shard cluster will have the same write throughput as a standalone instance.
- Most reads will tend to cluster on the same shard, assuming you access recent data more frequently.

Option 2: Shard by a semi-random key

To distribute data more evenly among the shards, you may consider using a more "random" piece of data, such as a hash of the `_id` field (i.e., the `ObjectId` as a shard key).

While this introduces some additional complexity into your application, to generate the key, it will distribute writes among the shards. In these deployments, having five shards will provide five times the write capacity as a single instance.

Using this shard key, or any hashed value as a key, presents the following downsides:

- The shard key, and the index on the key, will consume additional space in the database.
- Queries, unless they include the shard key itself, must run in parallel on all shards, which may lead to degraded performance.

This might be an acceptable trade-off in some situations. The workload of event logging systems tends to be heavily skewed toward writing; read performance may not be as critical as perfectly balanced write performance.

Option 3: Shard by an evenly distributed key in the data set

If a field in your documents has values that are evenly distributed among the documents, you should strongly consider using this key as a shard key.

Continuing the previous example, you might consider using the `path` field. This has a couple of advantages:

- Writes will tend to balance evenly among shards.
- Reads will tend to be selective and local to a single shard if the query selects on the `path` field.

The biggest potential drawback to this approach is that *all* hits to a particular `path` *must* go to the same chunk, and that chunk cannot be split by MongoDB, since all the documents in it have the same shard key. This might not be a problem if you have fairly even load on your website, but if one page gets a disproportionate number of hits, you can end up with a large chunk that is completely unsplittable that causes an unbalanced load on one shard.

 Test using your existing data to ensure that the distribution is truly even, and that there is a sufficient quantity of distinct values for the shard key.

Option 4: Shard by combining a natural and synthetic key

MongoDB supports compound shard keys that combine the best aspects of options 2 and 3. In these situations, the shard key would resemble { `path: 1 , ssk: 1` }, where `path` is an often-used natural key or value from your data and `ssk` is a hash of the `_id` field.

Using this type of shard key, data is largely distributed by the natural key, or `path`, which makes most queries that access the `path` field local to a single shard or group of shards. At the same time, if there is not sufficient distribution for specific values of `path`, the `ssk` makes it possible for MongoDB to create chunks that distribute data across the cluster.

In most situations, these kinds of keys provide the ideal balance between distributing writes across the cluster and ensuring that most queries will only need to access a select number of shards.

Test with your own data

Selecting shard keys is difficult because there are no definitive "best practices," the decision has a large impact on performance, and it is difficult or impossible to change the shard key after making the selection.

This section provides a good starting point for thinking about shard key selection. Nevertheless, the best way to select a shard key is to analyze the actual insertions and queries from your own application.

Although the details are beyond our scope here, you may also consider pre-splitting your chunks if your application has a very high and predictable insert pattern. In this case, you create empty chunks and manually pre-distribute them among your shard servers. Again, the best solution is to test with your own data.

Managing Event Data Growth

Without some strategy for managing the size of your database, an event logging system will grow indefinitely. This is particularly important in the context of MongoDB since MongoDB, as of the writing of this book, does not relinquish data to the filesystem, even when data gets removed from the database (i.e., the data files for your database will *never* shrink on disk). This section describes a few strategies to consider when managing event data growth.

Capped collections

Strategy: Depending on your data retention requirements as well as your reporting and analytics needs, you may consider using a *capped collection* to store your events. Capped collections have a fixed size, and drop old data automatically when inserting new data after reaching cap.

 In the current version, it is not possible to shard capped collections.

TTL collections

Strategy: If you want something *like* capped collections that *can* be sharded, you might consider using a "time to live" (TTL) index on that collection. If you define a TTL index on a collection, then periodically MongoDB will `remove()` old documents from the collection. To create a TTL index that will remove documents more than one hour old, for instance, you can use the following command:

```
>>> db.events.ensureIndex('time', expireAfterSeconds=3600)
```

Although TTL indexes are convenient, they do not possess the performance advantages of capped collections. Since TTL `remove()` operations aren't optimized beyond regular `remove()` operations, they may still lead to data fragmentation (capped collections are never fragmented) and still incur an index lookup on removal (capped collections don't require index lookups).

Multiple collections, single database

Strategy: Periodically rename your event collection so that your data collection rotates in much the same way that you might rotate logfiles. When needed, you can drop the oldest collection from the database.

This approach has several advantages over the single collection approach:

- Collection renames are fast and atomic.
- MongoDB does not bring any documents into memory to drop a collection.
- MongoDB can effectively reuse space freed by removing entire collections without leading to data fragmentation.

Nevertheless, this operation may increase some complexity for queries, if any of your analyses depend on events that may reside in the current and previous collection. For most real-time data-collection systems, this approach is ideal.

Multiple databases

Strategy: Rotate databases rather than collections, as was done in "Multiple collections, single database" (page 51).

While this *significantly* increases application complexity for insertions and queries, when you drop old databases MongoDB will return disk space to the filesystem. This approach makes the most sense in scenarios where your event insertion rates and/or your data retention rates were extremely variable.

For example, if you are performing a large backfill of event data and want to make sure that the entire set of event data for 90 days is available during the backfill, and during normal operations you only need 30 days of event data, you might consider using multiple databases.

Pre-Aggregated Reports

Although getting the event and log data into MongoDB efficiently and querying these log records is somewhat useful, higher-level aggregation is often much more useful in turning raw data into actionable information. In this section, we'll explore techniques to calculate and store pre-aggregated (or pre-canned) reports in MongoDB using incremental updates.

Solution Overview

This section outlines the basic patterns and principles for using MongoDB as an engine for collecting and processing events in real time for use in generating up-to-the-minute or up-to-the-second reports. We make the following assumptions about real-time analytics:

- You require up-to-the-minute data, or up-to-the-second if possible.
- The queries for ranges of data (by time) must be as fast as possible.
- Servers generating events that need to be aggregated have access to the MongoDB instance.

In particular, the scenario we'll explore here again uses data from a web server's access logs. Using this data, we'll pre-calculate reports on the number of hits to a collection of websites at various levels of granularity based on time (i.e., by minute, hour, day, week, and month) as well as by the path of a resource.

To achieve the required performance to support these tasks, we'll use MongoDB's *upsert* and *increment* operations to calculate statistics, allowing simple range-based queries to quickly return data to support time-series charts of aggregated data.

Schema Design

Schemas for real-time analytics systems must support simple and fast query and update operations. In particular, we need to avoid the following performance killers:

Individual documents growing significantly after they are created
> Document growth forces MongoDB to move the document on disk, slowing things down.

Collection scans
> The more documents that MongoDB has to examine to fulfill a query, the less efficient that query will be.

Documents with a large number (hundreds) of keys
> Due to the way MongoDB's internal document storage BSON stores documents, this can create wide variability in access time to particular values.

Intuitively, you may consider keeping "hit counts" in individual documents with one document for every unit of time (minute, hour, day, etc.). However, any query would then need to visit multiple documents for all nontrivial time-rage queries, which can slow overall query performance.

A better solution is to store a number of aggregate values in a single document, reducing the number of overall documents that the query engine must examine to return its results. The remainder of this section explores several schema designs that you might consider for this real-time analytics system, before finally settling on one that achieves both good update performance as well as good query performance.

One document per page per day, flat documents

Consider the following example schema for a solution that stores all statistics for a single day and page in a single document:

```
{
    _id: "20101010/site-1/apache_pb.gif",
    metadata: {
        date: ISODate("2000-10-10T00:00:00Z"),
        site: "site-1",
        page: "/apache_pb.gif" },
    daily: 5468426,
    hourly: {
        "0": 227850,
        "1": 210231,
        ...
        "23": 20457 },
```

```
        minute: {
            "0": 3612,
            "1": 3241,
            ...
            "1439": 2819 }
    }
```

This approach has a couple of advantages:

- For every request on the website, you only need to update one document.
- Reports for time periods within the day, for a single page, require fetching a single document.

If we use this schema, our real-time analytics system might record a hit with the following code:

```
def record_hit(collection, id, metadata, hour, minute):
    collection.update(
        { '_id': id,
          'metadata': metadata },
        { '$inc': {
            'daily': 1,
            'hourly.%d' % hour: 1,
            'minute.%d' % minute: 1 } },
        upsert=True)
```

This approach has the advantage of simplicity, since we can use MongoDB's "upsert" functionality to have the documents spring into existence as the hits are recorded.

There are, however, significant problems with this approach. The most significant issue is that as you add data into the hourly and monthly fields, the document grows. Although MongoDB will pad the space allocated to documents, it must still reallocate these documents multiple times throughout the day, which degrades performance, as shown in Figure 4-2.

The solution to this problem lies in *pre-allocating* documents with fields holding 0 values before the documents are actually used. If the documents have all their fields fully populated at pre-allocation time, the documents never grow and never need to be moved. Another benefit is that MongoDB will not add as much padding to the documents, leading to a more compact data representation and better memory and disk utilization.

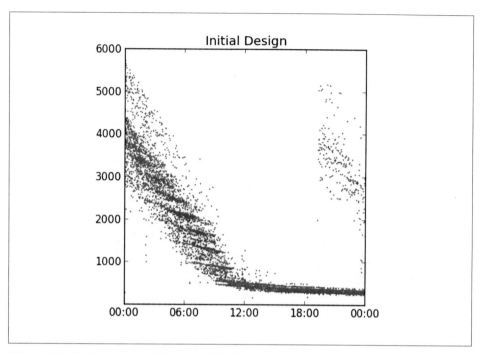

Figure 4-2. Performance with growing documents

One problem with our approach here, however, is that as we get toward the end of the day, the updates still become more expensive for MongoDB to perform, as shown in Figure 4-3. This is because MongoDB's internal representation of our minute property is actually an array of key-value pairs that it must scan sequentially to find the minute slot we're actually updating. So for the final minute of the day, MongoDB needs to examine 1,439 slots before actually finding the correct one to update. The solution to this is to build hierarchy into the minute property.

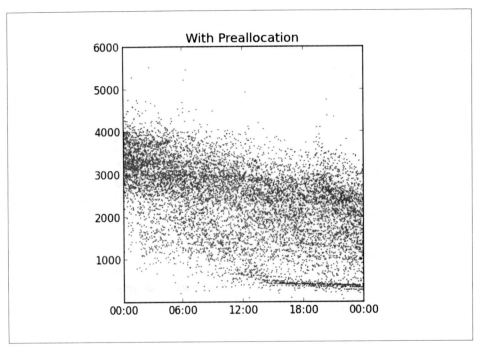

Figure 4-3. Performance with pre-allocated documents

One document per page per day, hierarchical documents

To optimize update and insert operations, we'll introduce some intra-document hierarchy. In particular, we'll split the minute field into 24 hourly fields:

```
{
    _id: "20101010/site-1/apache_pb.gif",
    metadata: {
        date: ISODate("2000-10-10T00:00:00Z"),
        site: "site-1",
        page: "/apache_pb.gif" },
    daily: 5468426,
    hourly: {
        "0": 227850,
        "1": 210231,
        ...
        "23": 20457 },
    minute: {
        "0": {
            "0": 3612,
            "1": 3241,
            ...
            "59": 2130 },
        "1": {
            "60": ... ,
```

```
        },
        ...
        "23": {
            ...
            "1439": 2819 }
        }
    }
```

This allows MongoDB to "skip forward" throughout the day when updating the minute data, which makes the update performance more uniform and faster later in the day, as shown in Figure 4-4.

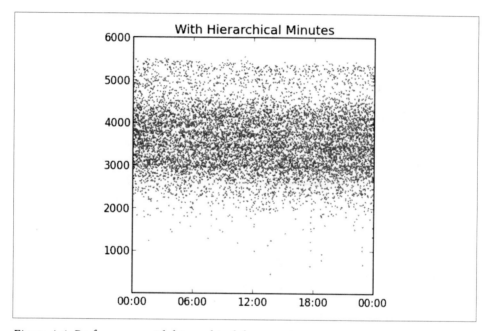

Figure 4-4. Performance with hierarchical documents

Separate documents by granularity level

Pre-allocation of documents helps our update speed significantly, but we still have a problem when querying data for long, multiday periods like months or quarters. In such cases, storing daily aggregates in a higher-level document can speed up these queries.

This introduces a second set of upsert operations to the data collection and aggregation portion of your application, but the gains in reduction of disk seeks on the queries should be worth the costs. Consider the example schema presented in Example 4-1 and Example 4-2.

Example 4-1. Daily statistics

```
{
    _id: "20101010/site-1/apache_pb.gif",
    metadata: {
        date: ISODate("2000-10-10T00:00:00Z"),
        site: "site-1",
        page: "/apache_pb.gif" },
    hourly: {
        "0": 227850,
        "1": 210231,
        ...
        "23": 20457 },
    minute: {
        "0": {
            "0": 3612,
            "1": 3241,
            ...
            "59": 2130 },
        "1": {
            "0": ...,
        },
        ...
        "23": {
            "59": 2819 }
    }
}
```

Example 4-2. Monthly statistics

```
{
    _id: "201010/site-1/apache_pb.gif",
    metadata: {
        date: ISODate("2000-10-00T00:00:00Z"),
        site: "site-1",
        page: "/apache_pb.gif" },
    daily: {
        "1": 5445326,
        "2": 5214121,
        ... }
}
```

To support this operation, our event logging operation adds a second `update` operation, which does slow down the operation, but the gains in query performance should be well worth it.

Operations

This section outlines a number of common operations for building and interacting with real-time analytics-reporting systems. The major challenge is in balancing read and write performance. All our examples here use the Python programming language and the pymongo driver, but you can implement this system using any language you choose.

Log an event

Logging an event such as a page request (i.e., "hit") is the main "write" activity for your system. To maximize performance, you'll be doing in-place updates with the up sert=True to create documents if they haven't been created yet. Consider the following example:

```
from datetime import datetime, time

def log_hit(db, dt_utc, site, page):

    # Update daily stats doc
    id_daily = dt_utc.strftime('%Y%m%d/') + site + page
    hour = dt_utc.hour
    minute = dt_utc.minute

    # Get a datetime that only includes date info
    d = datetime.combine(dt_utc.date(), time.min)
    query = {
        '_id': id_daily,
        'metadata': { 'date': d, 'site': site, 'page': page } }
    update = { '$inc': {
            'hourly.%d' % (hour,): 1,
            'minute.%d.%d' % (hour,minute): 1 } }
    db.stats.daily.update(query, update, upsert=True)

    # Update monthly stats document
    id_monthly = dt_utc.strftime('%Y%m/') + site + page
    day_of_month = dt_utc.day
    query = {
        '_id': id_monthly,
        'metadata': {
            'date': d.replace(day=1),
            'site': site,
            'page': page } }
    update = { '$inc': {
            'daily.%d' % day_of_month: 1} }
    db.stats.monthly.update(query, update, upsert=True)
```

The upsert operation (i.e., upsert=True) performs an update if the document exists, and an insert if the document does not exist.

If, for some reason, you need to determine whether an upsert was an insert or an update, you can always check the result of the update operation:

```
>>> result = db.foo.update({'x': 15}, {'$set': {'y': 5} }, upsert=True)
>>> result['updatedExisting']
False
>>> result = db.foo.update({'x': 15}, {'$set': {'y': 6} }, upsert=True)
>>> result['updatedExisting']
True
```

Pre-allocate

To prevent document growth, we'll pre-allocate new documents before the system needs them. In pre-allocation, we set all values to 0 so that documents don't need to grow to accommodate updates. Consider the following function:

```
def preallocate(db, dt_utc, site, page):

    # Get id values
    id_daily = dt_utc.strftime('%Y%m%d/') + site + page
    id_monthly = dt_utc.strftime('%Y%m/') + site + page

    # Get daily metadata
    daily_metadata = {
        'date': datetime.combine(dt_utc.date(), time.min),
        'site': site,
        'page': page }
    # Get monthly metadata
    monthly_metadata = {
        'date': daily_m['d'].replace(day=1),
        'site': site,
        'page': page }

    # Initial zeros for statistics
    daily_zeros = [
        ('hourly.%d' % h, 0) for i in range(24) ]
    daily_zeros += [
        ('minute.%d.%d' % (h,m), 0)
        for h in range(24)
        for m in range(60) ]
    monthly_zeros = [
        ('daily.%d' % d, 0) for d in range(1,32) ]

    # Perform upserts, setting metadata
    db.stats.daily.update(
        {
            '_id': id_daily,
            'metadata': daily_metadata
        },
        { '$inc': dict(daily_zeros) },
        upsert=True)
    db.stats.monthly.update(
```

```
{
    '_id': id_monthly,
    'daily': daily },
{ '$inc': dict(monthly_zeros) },
upsert=True)
```

This function pre-allocates both the monthly *and* daily documents at the same time. The performance benefits from separating these operations are negligible, so it's reasonable to keep both operations in the same function.

The question now arises as to *when* to pre-allocate the documents. Obviously, for best performance, they need to be pre-allocated before they are used (although the upsert code will actually work correctly even if it executes against a document that already exists). While we *could* pre-allocate the documents all at once, this leads to poor performance during the pre-allocation time. A better solution is to pre-allocate the documents probabilistically each time we log a hit:

```
from random import random
from datetime import datetime, timedelta, time

# Example probability based on 500k hits per day per page
prob_preallocate = 1.0 / 500000

def log_hit(db, dt_utc, site, page):
    if random.random() < prob_preallocate:
        preallocate(db, dt_utc + timedelta(days=1), site_page)
    # Update daily stats doc
    ...
```

Using this method, there will be a high probability that each document will already exist before your application needs to issue update operations. You'll also be able to prevent a regular spike in activity for pre-allocation, and be able to eliminate document growth.

Retrieving data for a real-time chart

This example describes fetching the data from the above MongoDB system for use in generating a chart that displays the number of hits to a particular resource over the last hour.

We can use the following query in a find_one operation at the Python console to retrieve the number of hits to a specific resource (i.e., /index.html) with minute-level granularity:

```
>>> db.stats.daily.find_one(
...     {'metadata': {'date':dt, 'site':'site-1', 'page':'/index.html'}},
...     { 'minute': 1 })
```

Alternatively, we can use the following query to retrieve the number of hits to a resource over the last day, with hour-level granularity:

```
code,sourceCode,pycon
>>> db.stats.daily.find_one(
...     {'metadata': {'date':dt, 'site':'site-1', 'page':'/foo.gif'}},
...     { 'hourly': 1 })
```

If we want a few days of hourly data, we can use a query in the following form:

```
>>> db.stats.daily.find(
...     {
...         'metadata.date': { '$gte': dt1, '$lte': dt2 },
...         'metadata.site': 'site-1',
...         'metadata.page': '/index.html'},
...     { 'metadata.date': 1, 'hourly': 1 } },
...     sort=[('metadata.date', 1)])
```

To support these query operations, we need to create a compound index on the following daily statistics fields: metadata.site, metadata.page, and metadata.date, in that order. This is because our queries have equality constraints on site and page, and a range query on date. To create the appropriate index, we can execute the following code:

```
>>> db.stats.daily.ensure_index([
...     ('metadata.site', 1),
...     ('metadata.page', 1),
...     ('metadata.date', 1)])
```

Get data for a historical chart

To retrieve daily data for a single month, we can use the following query:

```
>>> db.stats.monthly.find_one(
...     {'metadata':
...         {'date':dt,
...         'site': 'site-1',
...         'page':'/index.html'}},
...     { 'daily': 1 })
```

To retrieve several months of daily data, we can use a variation of the preceding query:

```
>>> db.stats.monthly.find(
...     {
...         'metadata.date': { '$gte': dt1, '$lte': dt2 },
...         'metadata.site': 'site-1',
...         'metadata.page': '/index.html'},
...     { 'metadata.date': 1, 'hourly': 1 } },
...     sort=[('metadata.date', 1)])
```

To execute these queries efficiently, we need an index on the monthly aggregate similar to the one we used for the daily aggregate:

```
>>> db.stats.monthly.ensure_index([
...     ('metadata.site', 1),
...     ('metadata.page', 1),
...     ('metadata.date', 1)])
```

This field order will efficiently support range queries for a single page over several months.

Sharding Concerns

Although the system as designed can support quite a large read and write load on a single-master deployment, sharding can further improve your performance and scalability. Your choice of shard key may depend on the precise workload of your deployment, but the choice of site-page is likely to perform well and lead to a well balanced cluster for most deployments.

To enable sharding for the daily and statistics collections, we can execute the following commands in the Python console:

```
>>> db.command('shardcollection', 'dbname.stats.daily', {
...       key : { 'metadata.site': 1, 'metadata.page' : 1 } })
{ "collectionsharded" : "dbname.stats.daily", "ok" : 1 }
>>> db.command('shardcollection', 'dbname.stats.monthly', {
...       key : { 'metadata.site': 1, 'metadata.page' : 1 } })
{ "collectionsharded" : "dbname.stats.monthly", "ok" : 1 }
```

One downside of the { metadata.site: 1, metadata.page: 1 } shard key is that if one page dominates all your traffic, all updates to that page will go to a single shard. This is basically unavoidable, since all updates for a single page are going to a single *document.*

You may wish to include the date in addition to the site and page fields so that MongoDB can split histories and serve different historical ranges with different shards. Note that this still does not solve the problem; all updates to a page will still go to one chunk, but historical queries will scale better.

To enable the three-part shard key, we just update our shardcollection with the new key:

```
>>> db.command('shardcollection', 'dbname.stats.daily', {
...       'key':{'metadata.site':1,'metadata.page':1,'metadata.date':1}})
{ "collectionsharded" : "dbname.stats.daily", "ok" : 1 }
>>> db.command('shardcollection', 'dbname.stats.monthly', {
...       'key':{'metadata.site':1,'metadata.page':1,'metadata.date':1}})
{ "collectionsharded" : "dbname.stats.monthly", "ok" : 1 }
```

Hierarchical Aggregation

Although the techniques of "Pre-Aggregated Reports" (page 52) can satisfy many operational intelligence system needs, it's often desirable to calculate statistics at multiple levels of abstraction. This section describes how we can use MongoDB's mapreduce command to convert transactional data to statistics at multiple layers of abstraction.

For clarity, this case study assumes that the incoming event data resides in a collection named events. This fits in well with "Storing Log Data" (page 37), making these two techniques work well together.

Solution Overview

The first step in the aggregation process is to aggregate event data into statistics at the finest required granularity. Then we'll use this aggregate data to generate the next least specific level granularity and repeat this process until we've generated all required views.

This solution uses several collections: the raw data (i.e., events) collection as well as collections for aggregated hourly, daily, weekly, monthly, and yearly statistics. All aggregations use the mapreduce database command in a hierarchical process. Figure 4-5 illustrates the input and output of each job.

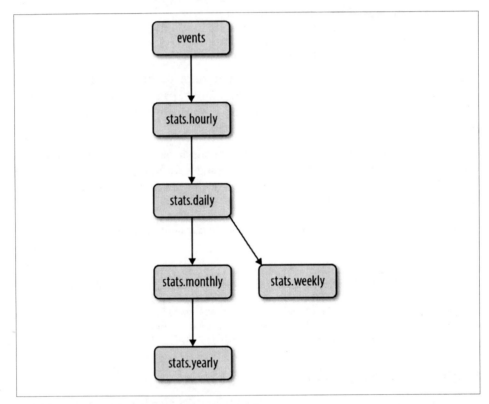

Figure 4-5. Hierarchical aggregation

Schema Design

When designing the schema for event storage, it's important to track the events included in the aggregation and events that are not yet included.

If you can batch your inserts into the events collection, you can use an autoincrement primary key by using the find_and_modify command to generate the _id values, as shown here:

```
>>> obj = db.my_sequence.find_and_modify(
...     query={'_id':0},
...     update={'$inc': {'inc': 50}}
...     upsert=True,
...     new=True)
>>> batch_of_ids = range(obj['inc']-50, obj['inc'])
```

However, in many cases you can simply include a timestamp with each event that you can use to distinguish processed events from unprocessed events.

This example assumes that you are calculating average session length for logged-in users on a website. The events will have the following form:

```
{
    "userid": "rick",
    "ts": ISODate('2010-10-10T14:17:22Z'),
    "length":95
}
```

The operations described here will calculate total and average session times for each user at the hour, day, week, month, and year. For each aggregation, we'll store the number of sessions so that MongoDB can incrementally recompute the average session times. The aggregate document will resemble the following:

```
{
    _id: { u: "rick", d: ISODate("2010-10-10T14:00:00Z") },
    value: {
        ts: ISODate('2010-10-10T15:01:00Z'),
        total: 254,
        count: 10,
        mean: 25.4 }
}
```

MapReduce

The MapReduce algorithm and its MongoDB implementation, the mapreduce command, is a popular way to process large amounts of data in bulk. If you're not familiar with MapReduce, the basics are illustrated in the following pseudocode:

```
from collections import defaultdict
def map_reduce(input, output, query, mapf, reducef, finalizef):
    # Map phase
```

```
    map_output = []
    for doc in input.find(output):
        map_output += mapf(doc) ❶

    # Shuffle phase
    map_output.sort() ❷
    docs_by_key = groupby_keys(map_output)

    # Reduce phase
    reduce_output = []
    for key, values in docs_by_key:
        reduce_output.append({
            '_id': key,
            'value': reducef(key, values) })

    # Finalize phase
    finalize_output = [] ❸
    for doc in reduce_output:
        key, value = doc['_id'], doc['value']
        reduce_output[key] = finalizef(key, value)

    output.remove() ❹
    output.insert(finalize_output)
```

❶ In MongoDB, mapf actually calls an emit function to generate zero or more documents to feed into the next phase. The signature of the mapf function is also modified to take no arguments, passing the document in the this JavaScript keyword.

❷ Sorting is not technically required; the purpose is to group documents with the same key together. Sorting is just one way to do this.

❸ Finalize is not required, but can be useful for computing things like mean values given a count and sum computed by the other parts of MapReduce.

❹ MongoDB provides several different options of how to store your output data. In this code, we're mimicking the output mode of replace.

The nice thing about this algorithm is that each of the phases can be run in parallel. In MongoDB, this benefit is somewhat limited by the presence, as of version 2.2, of a global JavaScript interpreter lock that forces all JavaScript in a single MongoDB process to run serially. Sharding allows you to get back some of this performance, but the full benefits of MapReduce still await the removal of the JavaScript lock from MongoDB.

Operations

This section assumes that all events exist in the events collection and have a timestamp. The operations are to aggregate from the events collection into the smallest aggregate —hourly totals—and then aggregate from the hourly totals into coarser granularity levels. In all cases, these operations will store aggregation time as a last_run variable.

Creating hourly views from event collections

To do our lowest-level aggregation, we need to first create a map function, as shown here:

```
mapf_hour = bson.Code('''function() {
    var key = {
        u: this.userid,
        d: new Date(
            this.ts.getFullYear(),
            this.ts.getMonth(),
            this.ts.getDate(),
            this.ts.getHours(),
            0, 0, 0);
    emit(
        key,
        {
            total: this.length,
            count: 1,
            mean: 0,
            ts: null });
}''')
```

In this case, mapf_hour emits key-value pairs that contain the data you want to aggregate, as you'd expect. The function also emits a ts value that makes it possible to cascade aggregations to coarser-grained aggregations (hour to day, etc.).

Next, we define the following reduce function:

```
reducef = bson.Code('''function(key, values) {
    var r = { total: 0, count: 0, mean: 0, ts: null };
    values.forEach(function(v) {
        r.total += v.total;
        r.count += v.count;
    });
    return r;
}''')
```

The reduce function returns a document in the same format as the output of the map function. This pattern for map and reduce functions makes MapReduce processes easier to test and debug.

While the reduce function ignores the `mean` and `ts` (timestamp) values, the finalize step, as follows, computes these data:

```
finalizef = bson.Code('''function(key, value) {
    if(value.count > 0) {
        value.mean = value.total / value.count;
    }
    value.ts = new Date();
    return value;
}''')
```

With the preceding functions defined, our actual `mapreduce` call resembles the following:

```
cutoff = datetime.utcnow() - timedelta(seconds=60)
query = { 'ts': { '$gt': last_run, '$lt': cutoff } }

db.events.map_reduce(
    map=mapf_hour,
    reduce=reducef,
    finalize=finalizef,
    query=query,
    out={ 'reduce': 'stats.hourly' })

last_run = cutoff
```

Output Modes

Here, we're using the `'reduce'` output mode. MongoDB's `mapreduce` provides several of these modes for different use cases:

replace
> In this mode, MongoDB will drop any collection that currently exists with the output name before writing the `mapreduce` results into it.

merge
> In this mode, MongoDB does not drop the output collection first, but will *overwrite* any existing results with the same key with the results of the `mapreduce` results.

reduce
> In this mode, MongoDB treats the output collection as additional input to the reduce phase. This mode is most useful for incremental aggregation, where we wish to *refine* existing results based on new data.

inline
> In this mode, no output collection is written; the results are returned as the result of the `mapreduce` command itself.

The cutoff variable allows you to process all events that have occurred since the last run but before one minute ago. This allows for some delay in logging events. You can safely run this aggregation as often as you like, provided that you update the last_run variable each time.

Since we'll be repeatedly querying the events collection by date, it's important to maintain an index on this property:

```
>>> db.events.ensure_index('ts')
```

Deriving day-level data

To calculate daily statistics, we can use the hourly statistics as input. We'll begin with the following map function:

```
mapf_day = bson.Code('''function() {
    var key = {
        u: this._id.u,
        d: new Date(
            this._id.d.getFullYear(),
            this._id.d.getMonth(),
            this._id.d.getDate(),
            0, 0, 0, 0) };
    emit(
        key,
        {
            total: this.value.total,
            count: this.value.count,
            mean: 0,
            ts: null });
}''')
```

The map function for deriving day-level data differs from this initial aggregation in the following ways:

- The aggregation key is the userid-date rather than userid-hour to support daily aggregation.

- The keys and values emitted (i.e., emit()) are actually the total and count values from the hourly aggregates, rather than properties from event documents.

This is the case for all the higher-level aggregation operations. Because the output of this map function is the same as the previous map function, we can actually use the same reduce and finalize functions. The actual code driving this level of aggregation is as follows:

```
cutoff = datetime.utcnow() - timedelta(seconds=60)
query = { 'value.ts': { '$gt': last_run, '$lt': cutoff } }

db.stats.hourly.map_reduce(
    map=mapf_day,
```

```
      reduce=reducef,
      finalize=finalizef,
      query=query,
      out={ 'reduce': 'stats.daily' })

   last_run = cutoff
```

There are a couple of things to note here. First of all, the query is not on `ts` now, but `value.ts`, the timestamp written during the finalization of the hourly aggregates. Also note that we are, in fact, aggregating from the `stats.hourly` collection into the `stats.daily` collection.

Because we'll be running this query on a regular basis, and the query depends on the `value.ts` field, we'll want to create an index on `value.ts`:

```
>>> db.stats.hourly.ensure_index('value.ts')
```

Weekly and monthly aggregation

We can use the aggregated day-level data to generate weekly and monthly statistics. A map function for generating weekly data follows:

```
mapf_week = bson.Code('''function() {
    var key = {
        u: this._id.u,
        d: new Date(
            this._id.d.valueOf()
            - dt.getDay()*24*60*60*1000) };
    emit(
        key,
        {
            total: this.value.total,
            count: this.value.count,
            mean: 0,
            ts: null });
}''')
```

Here, to get the group key, the function takes the current day and subtracts days until you get the beginning of the week. In the monthly map function, we'll use the first day of the month as the group key, as follows:

```
mapf_month = bson.Code('''function() {
        d: new Date(
            this._id.d.getFullYear(),
            this._id.d.getMonth(),
            1, 0, 0, 0, 0) };
    emit(
        key,
        {
            total: this.value.total,
            count: this.value.count,
            mean: 0,
```

```
        ts: null });
}''')
```

These map functions are identical to each other except for the date calculation.

To make our aggregation at these levels efficient, we need to create indexes on the value.ts field in each collection that serves as input to an aggregation:

```
>>> db.stats.daily.ensure_index('value.ts')
>>> db.stats.monthly.ensure_index('value.ts')
```

Refactor map functions

Using Python's string interpolation, we can refactor the map function definitions as follows:

```
mapf_hierarchical = '''function() {
    var key = {
        u: this._id.u,
        d: %s };
    emit(
        key,
        {
            total: this.value.total,
            count: this.value.count,
            mean: 0,
            ts: null });
}'''

mapf_day = bson.Code(
    mapf_hierarchical % '''new Date(
            this._id.d.getFullYear(),
            this._id.d.getMonth(),
            this._id.d.getDate(),
            0, 0, 0, 0)''')

mapf_week = bson.Code(
    mapf_hierarchical % '''new Date(
            this._id.d.valueOf()
            - dt.getDay()*24*60*60*1000)''')

mapf_month = bson.Code(
    mapf_hierarchical % '''new Date(
            this._id.d.getFullYear(),
            this._id.d.getMonth(),
            1, 0, 0, 0, 0)''')

mapf_year = bson.Code(
    mapf_hierarchical % '''new Date(
            this._id.d.getFullYear(),
            1, 1, 0, 0, 0, 0)''')
```

Now, we'll create an h_aggregate function to wrap the map_reduce operation to reduce code duplication:

```
def h_aggregate(icollection, ocollection, mapf, cutoff, last_run):
    query = { 'value.ts': { '$gt': last_run, '$lt': cutoff } }
    icollection.map_reduce(
        map=mapf,
        reduce=reducef,
        finalize=finalizef,
        query=query,
        out={ 'reduce': ocollection.name })
```

With h_aggregate defined, we can perform all aggregation operations as follows:

```
cutoff = datetime.utcnow() - timedelta(seconds=60)

# First step is still special
query = { 'ts': { '$gt': last_run, '$lt': cutoff } }
db.events.map_reduce(
    map=mapf_hour, reduce=reducef,
    finalize=finalizef, query=query,
    out={ 'reduce': 'stats.hourly' })

# But the other ones are not
h_aggregate(db.stats.hourly, db.stats.daily, mapf_day, cutoff, last_run)
h_aggregate(db.stats.daily, db.stats.weekly, mapf_week, cutoff, last_run)
h_aggregate(db.stats.daily, db.stats.monthly, mapf_month, cutoff, last_run)
h_aggregate(db.stats.monthly, db.stats.yearly, mapf_year, cutoff, last_run)

last_run = cutoff
```

As long as we save and restore the last_run variable between aggregations, we can run these aggregations as often as we like, since each aggregation operation is incremental (i.e., using output mode 'reduce').

Sharding Concerns

When sharding, we need to ensure that we don't choose the incoming timestamp as a shard key, but rather something that varies significantly in the most recent documents. In the previous example, we might consider using the userid as the most significant part of the shard key.

To prevent a single, active user from creating a large chunk that MongoDB cannot split, we'll use a compound shard key with username-timestamp on the events collection as follows:

```
>>> db.command('shardcollection','dbname.events', {
... 'key' : { 'userid': 1, 'ts' : 1} } )
{ "collectionsharded": "dbname.events", "ok" : 1 }
```

To shard the aggregated collections, we *must* use the _id field to work well with mapre
duce, so we'll issue the following group of shard operations in the shell:

```
>>> db.command('shardcollection', 'dbname.stats.daily', {
...        'key': { '_id': 1 } })
{ "collectionsharded": "dbname.stats.daily", "ok" : 1 }
>>> db.command('shardcollection', 'dbname.stats.weekly', {
...        'key': { '_id': 1 } })
{ "collectionsharded": "dbname.stats.weekly", "ok" : 1 }
>>> db.command('shardcollection', 'dbname.stats.monthly', {
...        'key': { '_id': 1 } })
{ "collectionsharded": "dbname.stats.monthly", "ok" : 1 }
>>> db.command('shardcollection', 'dbname.stats.yearly', {
...        'key': { '_id': 1 } })
{ "collectionsharded": "dbname.stats.yearly", "ok" : 1 }
```

We also need to update the h_aggregate MapReduce wrapper to support sharded output by adding 'sharded':True to the out argument. Our new h_aggregate now looks
like this:

```
def h_aggregate(icollection, ocollection, mapf, cutoff, last_run):
    query = { 'value.ts': { '$gt': last_run, '$lt': cutoff } }
    icollection.map_reduce(
        map=mapf,
        reduce=reducef,
        finalize=finalizef,
        query=query,
        out={ 'reduce': ocollection.name, 'sharded': True })
```

## CHAPTER 5

Ecommerce

In this chapter, we'll look at how MongoDB fits into the world of retail, particularly in two main areas: maintaining product catalog data and inventory management. Our first use case, "Product Catalog" (page 75), deals with the storage of product catalog data.

Our next use case, "Category Hierarchy" (page 84), examines the problem of maintaining a category hierarchy of product items in MongoDB.

The final use case in this chapter, "Inventory Management" (page 91), explores the use of MongoDB in an area a bit outside its traditional domain: managing inventory and checkout in an ecommerce system.

Product Catalog

In order to manage an ecommerce system, the first thing you need is a product catalog. Product catalogs must have the capacity to store many different types of objects with different sets of attributes. These kinds of data collections work quite well with MongoDB's flexible data model, making MongoDB a natural fit for this type of data.

Solution Overview

Before delving into the MongoDB solution, we'll examine the ways in which relational data models address the problem of storing products of various types. There have actually been several different approaches that address this problem, each with a different performance profile. This section examines some of the relational approaches and then describes the preferred MongoDB solution.

Concrete-table inheritance

One approach in a relational model is to create a table for each product category. Consider the following example SQL statement for creating database tables:

```
CREATE TABLE `product_audio_album` (
    `sku` char(8) NOT NULL,
    ...
    `artist` varchar(255) DEFAULT NULL,
    `genre_0` varchar(255) DEFAULT NULL,
    `genre_1` varchar(255) DEFAULT NULL,
    ...,
    PRIMARY KEY(`sku`))
...
CREATE TABLE `product_film` (
    `sku` char(8) NOT NULL,
    ...
    `title` varchar(255) DEFAULT NULL,
    `rating` char(8) DEFAULT NULL,
    ...,
    PRIMARY KEY(`sku`))
...
```

This approach has limited flexibility for two key reasons:

- You must create a new table for every new category of products.
- You must explicitly tailor all queries for the exact type of product.

Single-table inheritance

Another relational data model uses a single table for all product categories and adds new columns any time you need to store data regarding a new type of product. Consider the following SQL statement:

```
CREATE   TABLE `product` (
    `sku` char(8) NOT NULL,
    ...
    `artist` varchar(255) DEFAULT NULL,
    `genre_0` varchar(255) DEFAULT NULL,
    `genre_1` varchar(255) DEFAULT NULL,
    ...
    `title` varchar(255) DEFAULT NULL,
    `rating` char(8) DEFAULT NULL,
    ...,
    PRIMARY KEY(`sku`))
```

This approach is more flexible than concrete-table inheritance: it allows single queries to span different product types, but at the expense of space. It also continues to suffer from a lack of flexibility in that adding new types of product requires a potentially expensive ALTER TABLE operation.

Multiple-table inheritance

Another approach that's been used in relational modeling is multiple-table inheritance where you represent common attributes in a generic "product" table, with some variations in individual category product tables. Consider the following SQL statement:

```
CREATE TABLE `product` (
    `sku` char(8) NOT NULL,
    `title` varchar(255) DEFAULT NULL,
    `description` varchar(255) DEFAULT NULL,
    `price`, ...
    PRIMARY KEY(`sku`))

CREATE TABLE `product_audio_album` (
    `sku` char(8) NOT NULL,
    ...
    `artist` varchar(255) DEFAULT NULL,
    `genre_0` varchar(255) DEFAULT NULL,
    `genre_1` varchar(255) DEFAULT NULL,
    ...,
    PRIMARY KEY(`sku`),
    FOREIGN KEY(`sku`) REFERENCES `product`(`sku`))
...
CREATE TABLE `product_film` (
    `sku` char(8) NOT NULL,
    ...
    `title` varchar(255) DEFAULT NULL,
    `rating` char(8) DEFAULT NULL,
    ...,
    PRIMARY KEY(`sku`),
    FOREIGN KEY(`sku`) REFERENCES `product`(`sku`))
...
```

Multiple-table inheritance is more space-efficient than single-table inheritance and somewhat more flexible than concrete-table inheritance. However, this model does require an expensive JOIN operation to obtain all attributes relevant to a product.

Entity attribute values

The final substantive pattern from relational modeling is the entity-attribute-value (EAV) schema, where you would create a meta-model for product data. In this approach, you maintain a table with three columns (e.g., entity_id, attribute_id, and value), and these triples describe each product.

Consider the description of an audio recording. You may have a series of rows representing the following relationships:

Entity	Attribute	Value
sku_00e8da9b	type	Audio Album
sku_00e8da9b	title	A Love Supreme
sku_00e8da9b	...	...
sku_00e8da9b	artist	John Coltrane
sku_00e8da9b	genre	Jazz
sku_00e8da9b	genre	General
...	...	...

This schema is completely flexible:

- Any entity can have any set of any attributes.
- New product categories do not require *any* changes to the data model in the database.

There are, however, some significant problems with the EAV schema. One major issue is that all nontrivial queries require large numbers of JOIN operations. Consider retrieving the title, artist, and two genres for each item in the table:

```
SELECT entity,
    t0.value AS title,
    t1.value AS artist,
    t2.value AS genre0,
    t3.value as genre1
FROM eav AS t0
    LEFT JOIN eav AS t1 ON t0.entity = t1.entity
    LEFT JOIN eav AS t2 ON t0.entity = t2.entity
    LEFT JOIN eav AS t3 ON t0.entity = t3.entity;
```

And that's only bringing back four attributes! Another problem illustrated by this example is that the queries quickly become difficult to create and maintain.

Avoid modeling product data altogether

In addition to all the approaches just outlined, some ecommerce solutions with relational database systems skip relational modeling altogether, choosing instead to serialize all the product data into a BLOB column. Although the schema is simple, this approach makes sorting and filtering on any data embedded in the BLOB practically impossible.

The MongoDB answer

Because MongoDB is a nonrelational database, the data model for your product catalog can benefit from this additional flexibility. The best models use a single MongoDB collection to store all the product data, similar to the single-table inheritance model in "Single-table inheritance" (page 76).

Unlike single-table inheritance, however, MongoDB's dynamic schema means that the individual documents need not conform to the same rigid schema. As a result, each document contains only the properties appropriate to the particular class of product it describes.

At the beginning of the document, a document-based schema should contain general product information, to facilitate searches of the entire catalog. After the common fields, we'll add a `details` subdocument that contains fields that vary between product types. Consider the following example document for an album product:

```
{
  sku: "00e8da9b",
  type: "Audio Album",
  title: "A Love Supreme",
  description: "by John Coltrane",
  asin: "B0000A118M",

  shipping: {
    weight: 6,
    dimensions: {
      width: 10,
      height: 10,
      depth: 1
    },
  },

  pricing: {
    list: 1200,
    retail: 1100,
    savings: 100,
    pct_savings: 8
  },

  details: {
    title: "A Love Supreme [Original Recording Reissued]",
    artist: "John Coltrane",
    genre: [ "Jazz", "General" ],
        ...
    tracks: [
      "A Love Supreme, Part I: Acknowledgement",
      "A Love Supreme, Part II: Resolution",
      "A Love Supreme, Part III: Pursuance",
      "A Love Supreme, Part IV: Psalm"
    ],
  },
}
```

A movie item would have the same fields for general product information, shipping, and pricing, but different fields for the `details` subdocument. Consider the following:

```
{
  sku: "00e8da9d",
  type: "Film",
  ...,
  asin: "B000P0J0AQ",

  shipping: { ... },

  pricing: { ... },

  details: {
    title: "The Matrix",
    director: [ "Andy Wachowski", "Larry Wachowski" ],
    writer: [ "Andy Wachowski", "Larry Wachowski" ],
    ...,
    aspect_ratio: "1.66:1"
  },
}
```

Operations

For most deployments, the primary use of the product catalog is to perform search operations. This section provides an overview of various types of queries that may be useful for supporting an ecommerce site. Our examples use the Python programming language, but of course you can implement this system using any language you choose.

Find products sorted by percentage discount descending

Most searches will be for a particular type of product (album, movie, etc.), but in some situations you may want to return all products in a certain price range or discount percentage.

For example, the following query returns all products with a discount greater than 25%, sorted by descending percentage discount:

```
query = db.products.find( { 'pricing.pct_savings': {'$gt': 25 })
query = query.sort([('pricing.pct_savings', -1)])
```

To support this type of query, we'll create an index on the `pricing.pct_savings` field:

```
db.products.ensure_index('pricing.pct_savings')
```

 Since MongoDB can read indexes in ascending or descending order, the order of the index does not matter when creating single-element indexes.

Find albums by genre and sort by year produced

The following returns the documents for the albums of a specific genre, sorted in reverse chronological order:

```
query = db.products.find({
    'type':'Audio Album',
    'details.genre': 'jazz'})
query = query.sort([
    ('details.issue_date', -1)])
```

In order to support this query efficiently, we'll create a compound index on the properties used in the filter and the sort:

```
db.products.ensure_index([
    ('type', 1),
    ('details.genre', 1),
    ('details.issue_date', -1)])
```

 The final component of the index is the sort field. This allows MongoDB to traverse the index in the sorted order and avoid a slow in-memory sort.

Find movies based on starring actor

Another example of a detail field-based query would be one that selects films that a particular actor starred in, sorted by issue date:

```
query = db.products.find({'type': 'Film',
                          'details.actor': 'Keanu Reeves'})
query = query.sort([('details.issue_date', -1)])
```

To support this query, we'll create an index on the fields used in the query:

```
db.products.ensure_index([
    ('type', 1),
    ('details.actor', 1),
    ('details.issue_date', -1)])
```

This index begins with the type field and then narrows by the other search field, where the final component of the index is the sort field to maximize index efficiency.

Find movies with a particular word in the title

In most relational and document-based databases, querying for a single word within a string-type field requires scanning, making this query much less efficient than the others mentioned here.

One of the most-requested features of MongoDB is the so-called full-text index, which makes queries such as this one more efficient. In a full-text index, the individual words (sometimes even subwords) that occur in a field are indexed separately. In exciting and recent (as of the writing of this section) news, development builds of MongoDB currently contain a basic full-text search index, slated for inclusion in the next major release of MongoDB. Until MongoDB full-text search index shows up in a stable version of MongoDB, however, the best approach is probably deploying a separate full-text search engine (such as Apache Solr or ElasticSearch) alongside MongoDB, if you're going to be doing a lot of text-based queries.

Although there is currently no efficient full-text search support within MongoDB, there is support for using regular expressions (regexes) with queries. In Python, we can pass a compiled regex from the re module to the find() operation directly:

```
import re
re_hacker = re.compile(r'.*hacker.*', re.IGNORECASE)

query = db.products.find({'type': 'Film', 'title': re_hacker})
query = query.sort([('details.issue_date', -1)])
```

Although this query isn't particularly fast, there *is* a type of regex search that makes good use of the indexes that MongoDB *does* support: the prefix regex. Explicitly matching the beginning of the string, followed by a few prefix characters for the field you're searching for, allows MongoDB to use a "regular" index efficiently:

```
import re
re_prefix = re.compile(r'^A Few Good.*')

query = db.products.find({'type': 'Film', 'title': re_prefix})
query = query.sort([('details.issue_date', -1)])
```

In this query, since we've matched the *prefix* of the title, MongoDB can seek directly to the titles we're interested in.

 Regular Expression Pitfalls

If you use the re.IGNORECASE flag, you're basically back where you were, since the indexes are created as case-sensitive. If you want case-insensitive search, it's typically a good idea to store the data you want to search on in all-lowercase or all-uppercase format.

If for some reason you *don't* want to use a compiled regular expression, MongoDB provides a special syntax for regular expression queries using plain Python dict objects:

```
query = db.products.find({
    'type': 'Film',
    'title': {'$regex': '.*hacker.*', '$options':'i'}})
query = query.sort([('details.issue_date', -1)])
```

The indexing strategy for these kinds of queries is different from previous attempts. Here, create an index on { `type: 1, details.issue_date: -1, title: 1` } using the following Python console:

```
>>> db.products.ensure_index([
...        ('type', 1),
...        ('details.issue_date', -1),
...        ('title', 1)])
```

This index makes it possible to avoid scanning whole documents by using the index for scanning the title rather than forcing MongoDB to scan whole documents for the title field. Additionally, to support the sort on the `details.issue_date` field, by placing this field *before* the `title` field, ensures that the result set is already ordered before MongoDB filters title field.

Conclusion: Index all the things!

In ecommerce systems, we typically *don't* know exactly what the user will be filtering on, so it's a good idea to create a number of indexes on queries that are likely to happen. Although such indexing *will* slow down updates, a product catalog is only very infrequently updated, so this drawback is justified by the significant improvements in search speed. To sum up, if your application has a code path to execute a query, there should be an index to accelerate that query.

Sharding Concerns

Database performance for these kinds of deployments are dependent on indexes. You may use sharding to enhance performance by allowing MongoDB to keep larger portions of those indexes in RAM. In sharded configurations, you should select a shard key that allows the server to route queries directly to a single shard or small group of shards.

Since most of the queries in this system include the `type` field, it should be included in the shard key. Beyond this, the remainder of the shard key is difficult to predict without information about your database's actual activity and distribution. There are a few things we can say *a priori*, however:

- `details.issue_date` would be a poor addition to the shard key because, although it appears in a number of queries, no query was *selective* by this field, so `mongos` would not be able to route such queries based on the shard key.

- It's good to ensure some fields from the `detail` document that are frequently queried, as well as some with an even distribution to prevent large unsplittable chunks.

In the following example, we've assumed that the `details.genre` field is the second-most queried field after `type`. To enable sharding on these fields, we'll use the following `shardcollection` command:

```
>>> db.command('shardcollection', 'dbname.product', {
...     key : { 'type': 1, 'details.genre' : 1, 'sku':1 } })
{ "collectionsharded" : "dbname.product", "ok" : 1 }
```

Scaling read performance without sharding

While sharding is the best way to scale operations, some data sets make it impossible to partition data so that mongos can route queries to specific shards. In these situations, mongos sends the query to all shards and then combines the results before returning to the client.

In these situations, you can gain some additional read performance by allowing mongos to read from the secondary mongod instances in a replica set by configuring the read preference in the client. Read preference is configurable on a per-connection or per-operation basis. In pymongo, this is set using the read_preference keyword argument.

The pymongo.SECONDARY argument in the following example permits reads from the secondary (as well as a primary) for the entire connection:

```
conn = pymongo.MongoClient(read_preference=pymongo.SECONDARY_PREFERRED)
```

If you wish to restrict reads to *only* occur on the secondary, you can use SECONDARY instead:

```
conn = pymongo.MongoClient(read_preference=pymongo.SECONDARY)
```

You can also specify read_preference for specific queries, as shown here:

```
results = db.product.find(..., read_preference=pymongo.SECONDARY_PREFERRED)
```

Or:

```
results = db.product.find(..., read_preference=pymongo.SECONDARY)
```

Category Hierarchy

One of the issues faced by product catalog maintainers is the classification of products. Products are typically classified hierarchically to allow for convenient catalog browsing and product planning. One question that arises is just what to do when that categorization changes. This use case addresses the construction and maintenance of a hierarchical classification system in MongoDB.

Solution Overview

To model a product category hierarchy, our solution here keeps each category in its own document with a list of the ancestor categories for that particular subcategory. To anchor our examples, we use music genres as the categorization scheme we'll examine.

Since the hierarchical categorization of products changes relatively infrequently, we're more concerned here with query performance and update consistency than update performance.

Schema Design

Our schema design will focus on the hierarchy in Figure 5-1. When designing a hierarchical schema, one approach would be to simply store a `parent_id` in each document:

```
{ _id: "modal-jazz",
  name: "Modal Jazz",
  parent: "bop",
  ...
}
```

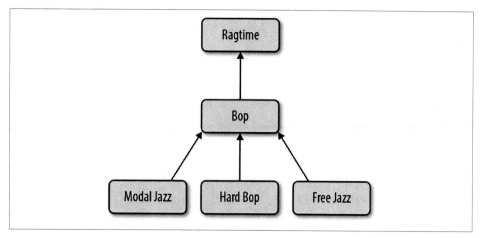

Figure 5-1. A music classification hierarchy

While using such a schema is flexible, it only allows us to examine one level of hierarchy with any given query. If we want to be able to instead query for all ancestors or descendants of a category, it's better to store the ancestor list in some way.

One approach to this would be to construct the ID of a subcategory based on the IDs of its parent categories:

```
{ _id: "ragtime:bop:modal-jazz",
  name: "Modal Jazz",
  parent: "ragtime/bop",
  ...
}
```

This is a convenient approach because:

- The ancestors of a particular category are self-evident from the `_id` field.

- The descendants of a particular category can be easily queried by using a prefix-style regular expression. For instance, to find all descendants of "bop," you would use a query like {_id: /^ragtime:bop:.*/}.

There are a couple of problems with this approach, however:

- Displaying the ancestors for a category requires a second query to return the ancestor documents.
- Updating the hierarchy is cumbersome, requiring string manipulation of the _id field.

The solution we've chosen here is to store the ancestors as an embedded array, including the name of each ancestor for display purposes. We've also switched to using ObjectId()s for the _id field and moving the human-readable slug to its own field to facilitate changing the slug if necessary. Our final schema, then, looks like the following:

```
{ _id: ObjectId(...),
  slug: "modal-jazz",
  name: "Modal Jazz",
  parent: ObjectId(...),
  ancestors: [
    { _id: ObjectId(...),
      slug: "bop",
      name: "Bop" },
    { _id: ObjectId(...),
      slug: "ragtime",
      name: "Ragtime" } ] }
```

Operations

This section outlines the category hierarchy manipulations that you may need in an ecommerce site. All examples in this document use the Python programming language and the pymongo driver for MongoDB, but of course you can implement this system using any supported programming language.

Read and display a category

The most basic operation is to query a category hierarchy based on a slug. This type of query is often used in an ecommerce site to generate a list of "breadcrumbs" displaying to the user just where in the hierarchy they are while browsing. The query, then, is the following:

```
category = db.categories.find(
    {'slug': slug },
    {'_id': 0, 'name': 1, 'ancestors.slug': 1, 'ancestors.name': 1} )
```

In order to make this query fast, we just need an index on the slug field:

```
>>> db.categories.ensure_index('slug', unique=True)
```

Add a category to the hierarchy

Suppose we wanted to modify the hierarchy by adding a new category, as shown in Figure 5-2. This insert operation would be trivial if we had used our *simple* schema that only stored the parent ID:

```
doc = dict(name='Swing', slug='swing', parent=ragtime_id)
```

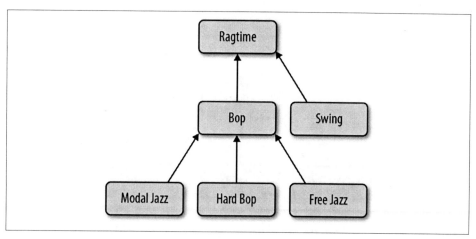

Figure 5-2. Adding Swing to the hierarchy

Since we are keeping information on *all* the ancestors, however, we need to actually calculate this array and store it after performing the insert. For this, we'll define the following build_ancestors helper function:

```
def build_ancestors(_id, parent_id):
    parent = db.categories.find_one(
        {'_id': parent_id},
        {'name': 1, 'slug': 1, 'ancestors':1})
    parent_ancestors = parent.pop('ancestors')
    ancestors = [ parent ] + parent_ancestors
    db.categories.update(
        {'_id': _id},
        {'$set': { 'ancestors': ancestors } })
```

Note that you only need to travel up one level in the hierarchy to get the ancestor list for "Ragtime" that you can use to build the ancestor list for "Swing." Once you have the parent's ancestors, you can build the full ancestor list trivially. Putting it all together then, let's insert a new category:

```
doc = dict(name='Swing', slug='swing', parent=ragtime_id)
swing_id = db.categories.insert(doc)
build_ancestors(swing_id, ragtime_id)
```

Change the ancestry of a category

This section addresses the process for reorganizing the hierarchy by moving "Bop" under "Swing," as shown in Figure 5-3. First, we'll update the bop document to reflect the change in its ancestry:

```
db.categories.update(
    {'_id':bop_id}, {'$set': { 'parent': swing_id } } )
```

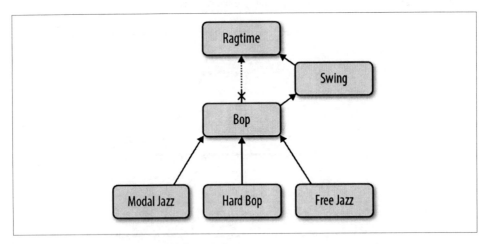

Figure 5-3. Adding Swing to the hierarchy

Now we need to update the ancestor list of the bop document *and all its descendants*. In order to do this, we'll first build the subgraph of bop in memory, including all of the descendants of bop, and then calculate and store the ancestor list for each node in the subgraph.

For the purposes of calculating the ancestor list, we will store the subgraph in a dict containing all the nodes in the subgraph, keyed by their parent field. This will allow us to quickly traverse the hierarchy, starting with the bop node and visiting the nodes in order:

```
from collections import defaultdict

def build_subgraph(root):
    nodes = db.categories.find(
        { 'ancestors._id': root['_id'] },
        { 'parent': 1, 'name': 1, 'slug': 1, 'ancestors': 1})
    nodes_by_parent = defaultdict(list)  ❶
    for n in nodes:
        nodes_py_parent[n['parent']].append(n)
    return nodes_by_parent
```

❶ The defaultdict from the Python standard library is a dictionary with a special behavior when you try to access a key that is not there. In this case, rather than raising a KeyError like a regular dict, it will generate a new value based on a factory function passed to its constructor. In this case, we're using the list function to create an empty list when the given parent isn't found.

Once we have this subgraph, we can update the nodes as follows:

```
def update_node_and_descendants(
    nodes_by_parent, node, parent):

    # Update node's ancestors
    node['ancestors'] = parent.ancestors + [
        { '_id': parent['_id'],
          'slug': parent['slug'],
          'name': parent['name']} ]
    db.categories.update(
        {'_id': node['_id']},
        {'$set': {
            'ancestors': ancestors,
            'parent': parent['_id'] } })

    # Recursively call children of 'node'
    for child in nodes_by_parent[node['_id']]:
        update_node_and_descendants(
            nodes_by_parent, child, node)
```

In order to ensure that the subgraph-building operation is fast, we'll need an index on the ancestors._id field:

```
>>> db.categories.ensure_index('ancestors._id')
```

Rename a category

One final operation we'll explore with our category hierarchy is renaming a category. In order to a rename a category, we'll need to both update the category itself and also update all its descendants. Consider renaming "Bop" to "BeBop," as in Figure 5-4.

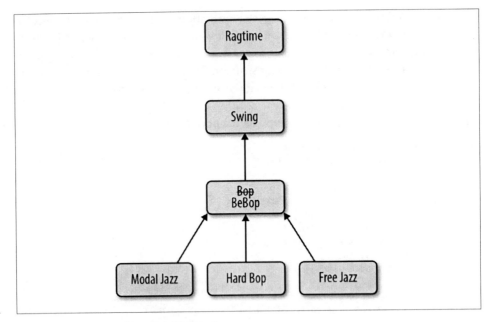

Figure 5-4. Rename "Bop" to "BeBop"

First, we'll update the category name with the following operation:

```
db.categories.update(
    {'_id':bop_id}, {'$set': { 'name': 'BeBop' } } )
```

Next, we'll update each descendant's ancestors list:

```
db.categories.update(
    {'ancestors._id': bop_id},
    {'$set': { 'ancestors.$.name': 'BeBop' } },
    multi=True)
```

There are a couple of things to know about this update:

- We've used the positional operation $ to match the exact "ancestor" entry that matches the query.

- The `multi` option allows us to update all documents that match this query. By default, MongoDB will only update the first document that matches.

Sharding Concerns

For most deployments, sharding the categories collection has limited value because the collection itself will have a small number of documents. If you *do* need to shard, since all the queries use _id, it makes an appropriate shard key:

```
>>> db.command('shardcollection', 'dbname.categories', {
...     'key': {'_id': 1} })
{ "collectionsharded" : "dbname.categories", "ok" : 1 }
```

Inventory Management

The most basic requirement of an ecommerce system is its checkout functionality. Beyond the basic ability to fill up a shopping cart and pay, customers have come to expect online ordering to account for out-of-stock conditions, not allowing them to place items in their shopping cart unless those items are, in fact, available. This section provides an overview of an integrated shopping cart and inventory management data model for an online store.

Solution Overview

Customers in ecommerce stores regularly add and remove items from their "shopping cart," change quantities multiple times, abandon the cart at any point, and sometimes have problems during and after checkout that require a hold or canceled order. These activities make it difficult to maintain inventory systems and counts and to ensure that customers cannot "buy" items that are unavailable while they shop in your store.

The solution presented here maintains the traditional metaphor of the shopping cart, but allows inactive shopping carts to *age*. After a shopping cart has been inactive for a certain period of time, all items in the cart re-enter the available inventory and the cart is emptied. The various states that a shopping cart can be in, then, are summarized in Figure 5-5.

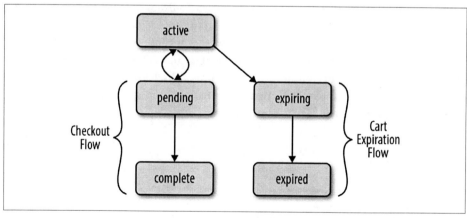

Figure 5-5. Shopping cart states

Here's an explanation of each state:

active
> In this state, the user is active and items may be added or removed from the shopping cart.

pending
> In this state, the cart is being checked out, but payment has not yet been captured. Items may not be added or removed from the cart at this time.

expiring
> In this state, the cart has been inactive for too long and it is "locked" while its items are returned to available inventory.

expired
> In this state, the shopping cart is inactive and unavailable. If the user returns, a new cart must be created.

Schema

Our schema for this portion of the system consists of two collections: `product` and `cart`. Let's consider `product` first. This collection contains one document for each item a user can place in their cart, called a "stock-keeping unit" or SKU. The simplest approach is to simply use a SKU number as the `_id` and keep a `quantity` counter for each item. We'll add in a `details` field for any item details you wish to display to the user as they're browsing the store:

```
{ _id: '00e8da9b', qty: 16, details: ... }
```

It turns out to be useful to augment this schema with a list of shopping carts containing the particular SKU. We do this because we're going to use `product` as the definitive *collection of record* for our system. This means that if there is ever a case where `cart` and `product` contain inconsistent data, `product` is the collection that "wins." Since MongoDB does not support multidocument transactions, it's important to have a method of "cleaning up" when two collections become inconsistent, and keeping a `carted` property in `product` provides that avenue here:

```
{ _id: '00e8da9b',
  qty: 16,
  carted: [
    { qty: 1, cart_id: 42,
      timestamp: ISODate("2012-03-09T20:55:36Z"), },
    { qty: 2, cart_id: 43,
      timestamp: ISODate("2012-03-09T21:55:36Z") }
  ]
}
```

In this case, the inventory shows that we actually have 16 available items, but there are also two carts that have not yet completed checkout, which have one and two items in them, respectively.

Our `cart` collection, then, would contain an `_id`, `state`, `last_modified` date to handle expiration, and a list of items and quantities:

```
{ _id: 42,
  last_modified: ISODate("2012-03-09T20:55:36Z"),
  status: 'active',
  items: [
    { sku: '00e8da9b', qty: 1, details: {...} },
    { sku: '0ab42f88', qty: 4, details: {...} }
  ]
}
```

Note that we've copied the item details from the `product` document into the `cart` document so we can display relevant details for each line item without fetching the original `product` document. This also helps us avoid the usability problem of what to do about a SKU that changes prices between being added to the cart and checking out; in this case, we always charge the user the price *at the time the item was added to the cart.*

Operations

This section introduces operations that we'll want to support on our data model. As always, the examples use the Python programming language and the pymongo driver, but the system can be implemented in any language you choose.

Add an item to a shopping cart

Moving an item from the available inventory to a cart is a fundamental requirement for a shopping cart system. Our system must ensure that an item is never added to a shopping cart unless there is sufficient inventory to fulfill the order.

Patterns

For this operation, and for several others in this section, we'll use patterns from Chapter 3 to keep our `product` and `cart` collections consistent.

In order to add an item to our cart, the basic approach will be to:

1. Update the cart, ensuring it is still active, and adding the line item.
2. Update the inventory, decrementing available stock, *only if there is sufficient inventory available.*

3. If the inventory update failed due to lack of inventory, *compensate* by rolling back our cart update and raising an exception to the user.

The actual function we write to add an item to a cart would resemble the following:

```
def add_item_to_cart(cart_id, sku, qty, details):
    now = datetime.utcnow()

    # Make sure the cart is still active and add the line item
    result = db.cart.update(
        {'_id': cart_id, 'status': 'active' },
        { '$set': { 'last_modified': now },
          '$push': {
              'items': {'sku': sku, 'qty':qty, 'details': details } } })
    if not result['updatedExisting']:
        raise CartInactive()

    # Update the inventory
    result = db.product.update(
        {'_id':sku, 'qty': {'$gte': qty}}, ❶
        {'$inc': {'qty': -qty},
          '$push': {
              'carted': { 'qty': qty, 'cart_id':cart_id,
                          'timestamp': now } } }) ❷
    if not result['updatedExisting']:
        # Roll back our cart update
        db.cart.update(
            {'_id': cart_id },
            { '$pull': { 'items': {'sku': sku } } }) ❸
        raise InadequateInventory()
```

❶ Here, we're using the quantity in our `update` spec to ensure that only a document with both the right SKU *and* sufficient inventory can be updated. Once again, we use `safe` mode to have the server tell us if anything was updated.

❷ Note that we need to update the `carted` property as well as `qty` when modifying product.

❸ Here, we `$pull` the just-added item from the cart. Note that `$pull` means that *all* line items for the SKU will be pulled. This is not a problem for us, since we'll introduce another function to modify the quantity of a SKU in the cart.

Since our updates always include `_id`, and this is a unique and indexed field, no additional indexes are necessary to make this function perform well.

Modifying the quantity in the cart

Often, a user will wish to modify the quantity of a particular SKU in their cart. Our system needs to ensure that when a user increases the quantity of an item, there is sufficient inventory. Additionally, the `carted` attribute in the `product` collection needs to be updated to reflect the new quantity in the cart.

Our basic approach here is the same as when adding a new line item:

1. Update the cart (optimistically assuming there is sufficient inventory).

2. Update the `product` collection *if there is sufficient inventory.*

3. Roll back the cart update if there is insufficient inventory and raise an exception.

Our code, then, looks like the following:

```
def update_quantity(cart_id, sku, old_qty, new_qty):
    now = datetime.utcnow()
    delta_qty = new_qty - old_qty

    # Make sure the cart is still active and add the line item
    result = db.cart.update(
        {'_id': cart_id, 'status': 'active', 'items.sku': sku }, ❶
        {'$set': { 'last_modified': now },
         '$inc': { 'items.$.qty': delta_qty } ❷
        })
    if not result['updatedExisting']:
        raise CartInactive()

    # Update the inventory
    result = db.product.update(
        {'_id':sku,
         'carted.cart_id': cart_id, ❸
         'qty': {'$gte': delta_qty} },
        {'$inc': {'qty': -delta_qty },
         '$set': { 'carted.$.qty': new_qty, 'timestamp': now } })
    if not result['updatedExisting']:
        # Roll back our cart update
        db.cart.update(
            {'_id': cart_id, 'items.sku': sku },
            {'$inc': { 'items.$.qty': -delta_qty } }) ❹
        raise InadequateInventory()
```

❶ Note that we're including `items.sku` in our update spec. This allows us to use the positional `$` in our `$set` modifier to update the correct (matching) line item.

❷❸ Both here and in the rollback operation, we're using the `$inc` modifier rather than `$set` to update the quantity. This allows us to correctly handle situations where a user might be updating the cart multiple times simultaneously (say, in two different browser windows).

❹ Here again, we're using the positional `$` in our update to `carted`, so we need to include the `cart_id` in our update spec.

Once again, we're using _id in all our updates, so adding an index doesn't help us here.

Checking out

The checkout operation needs to do two main operations:

- Capture payment details.
- Update the carted items once payment is made.

Our basic algorithm here is as follows:

1. Lock the cart by setting it to pending status.

2. Collect payment for the cart. If this fails, unlock the cart by setting it back to active status.

3. Set the cart's status to complete.

4. Remove all references to this cart from any carted properties in the product collection.

The code would look something like the following:

```
def checkout(cart_id):
    now = datetime.utcnow()

    result = db.cart.update( ❶
        {'_id': cart_id, 'status': 'active' },
        update={'$set': { 'status': 'pending','last_modified': now } } )
    if not result['updatedExisting']:
        raise CartInactive()

    try:
        collect_payment(cart)
    except:
        db.cart.update(
            {'_id': cart_id },
            {'$set': { 'status': 'active' } } )
        raise
    db.cart.update(
        {'_id': cart_id },
        {'$set': { 'status': 'complete' } } )
    db.product.update(
        {'carted.cart_id': cart_id},
        {'$pull': {'cart_id': cart_id} },
        multi=True) ❷
```

❶   We're using the return value from update here to let us know whether we actually *locked* a currently *active* cart by moving it to *pending* status.

❷ We're using `multi=True` here to ensure that *all* the SKUs that were in the cart have their `carted` properties updated.

Here, we could actually use a new index on the `carted.cart_id` property so that our final `update` is fast:

```
>>> db.product.ensure_index('carted.cart_id')
```

Returning inventory from timed-out carts

Periodically, we need to "expire" inactive carts and return their items to available inventory. Our approach here is as follows:

1. Find all carts that are older than the `threshold` and are due for expiration. Lock them by setting their status to `"expiring"`.

2. For each `"expiring"` cart, return all their items to available inventory.

3. Once the `product` collection has been updated, set the cart's status to `"expired"`.

The actual code, then, looks something like the following:

```
def expire_carts(timeout):
    now = datetime.utcnow()
    threshold = now - timedelta(seconds=timeout)

    # Lock and find all the expiring carts
    db.cart.update(
        {'status': 'active', 'last_modified': { '$lt': threshold } },
        {'$set': { 'status': 'expiring' } },
        multi=True )  ❶

    # Actually expire each cart
    for cart in db.cart.find({'status': 'expiring'}):  ❷

        # Return all line items to inventory
        for item in cart['items']:
            db.product.update(  ❸
                { '_id': item['sku'],
                  'carted.cart_id': cart['id'] },
                {'$inc': { 'qty': item['qty'] },
                 '$pull': { 'carted': { 'cart_id': cart['id'] } } }) <
        db.cart.update(  ❹
            {'_id': cart['id'] },
            {'$set': { status': 'expired' })
```

❶ We're using `multi=True` to "batch up" our cart expiration initial lock.

❷   Unfortunately, we need to handle expiring the carts individually, so this function can actually be somewhat time-consuming. Note, however, that the `ex pire_carts` function is safely resumable, since we have effectively "locked" the carts needing expiration by placing them in `"expiring"` status.

❸   Here, we update the inventory, but only if it still has a `carted` entry for the cart we're expiring. Note that without the `carted` property, our function would become unsafe to retry if an exception occurred since the inventory could be incremented multiple times for a single cart.

❹   Finally, we fully expire the cart. We could also `delete` it here if we don't wish to keep it around any more.

In order to support returning inventory from timed-out carts, we'll need to create an index on the `status` and `last_modified` properties. Since our query on `last_modi fied` is an inequality, we should place it last in the compound index:

```
>>> db.cart.ensure_index([('status', 1), ('last_modified', 1)])
```

Error handling

The previous operations do not account for one possible failure situation. If an exception occurs after updating the shopping cart but before updating the inventory collection, then we have an inconsistent situation where there is inventory "trapped" in a shopping cart.

To account for this case, we'll need a periodic cleanup operation that finds inventory items that have `carted` items and check to ensure that they exist in some user's active cart, and return them to available inventory if they do not. Our approach here is to visit each `product` with some `carted` entry older than a specified timestamp. Then, for each SKU found:

1. Load the `cart` that's possibly expired. If it's actually `"active"`, refresh the `carted` entry in the `product`.

2. If an `"active"` cart was not found to match the `carted` entry, then the `carted` is removed and the available inventory is updated:

```
def cleanup_inventory(timeout):
    now = datetime.utcnow()
    threshold = now - timedelta(seconds=timeout)

    # Find all the expiring carted items
    for item in db.product.find( ❶
        {'carted.timestamp': {'$lt': threshold }}):

        # Find all the carted items that matched
        carted = dict(
```

```
                    (carted_item['cart_id'], carted_item)
                    for carted_item in item['carted']
                    if carted_item['timestamp'] < threshold)

            # First Pass: Find any carts that are active and refresh the carted
            #    items
            for cart in db.cart.find(
                { '_id': {'$in': carted.keys() },
                'status':'active'}):
                cart = carted[cart['_id']]

                db.product.update( ❷
                    { '_id': item['_id'],
                     'carted.cart_id': cart['_id'] },
                    { '$set': {'carted.$.timestamp': now } })
                del carted[cart['_id']]

            # Second Pass: All the carted items left in the dict need to now be
            #    returned to inventory
            for cart_id, carted_item in carted.items():
                db.product.update( ❸
                    { '_id': item['_id'],
                     'carted.cart_id': cart_id },
                    { '$inc': { 'qty': carted_item['qty'] },
                     '$pull': { 'carted': { 'cart_id': cart_id } } })
```

❶ Here, we're visiting each SKU that has possibly expired carted entries one at a time. This has the potential for being time-consuming, so the timeout value should be chosen to keep the number of SKUs returned small. In particular, this timeout value should be greater than the timeout value used when expiring carts.

❷ Note that we're once again using the positional $ to update only the carted item we're interested in. Also note that we're *not* just updating the product document in-memory and calling .save(), as that can lead to race conditions.

❸ Here again we don't call .save(), since the product's quantity may have been updated since this function started executing. Also note that we might end up modifying the same product document multiple times (once for each possibly expired carted entry). This is most likely not a problem, as we expect this code to be executed extremely infrequently.

Here, the index we need is on carted.timestamp to make the initial find() run quickly:

```
>>> db.product.ensure_index('carted.timestamp')
```

Sharding Concerns

If you need to shard the data for this system, the _id field is a reasonable choice for shard key since most updates use the _id field in their spec, allowing mongos to route each update to a single mongod process. There are a couple of potential drawbacks with using _id, however:

- If the cart collection's _id is an increasing value such as an ObjectId(), all new carts end up on a single shard.

- Cart expiration and inventory adjustment require update operations and queries to broadcast to all shards when using _id as a shard key.

It's possible to mitigate the first problem at least by using a pseudorandom value for _id when creating a cart. A reasonable approach would be the following:

```
import hashlib
import bson

def new_cart():
    object_id = bson.ObjectId() ❶
    cart_id = hashlib.md5(str(object_id)).hexdigest() ❷
    return cart_id
```

❶   We're creating a bson.ObjectId() to get a unique value to use in our hash. Note that since ObjectId uses the current timestamp as its most significant bits, it's not an appropriate choice for shard key.

❷   Now we randomize the object_id, creating a string that is *extremely likely* to be unique in our system.

To actually perform the sharding, we'd execute the following commands:

```
>>> db.command('shardcollection', 'dbname.inventory'
...             'key': { '_id': 1 } )
{ "collectionsharded" : "dbname.inventory", "ok" : 1 }
>>> db.command('shardcollection', 'dbname.cart')
...             'key': { '_id': 1 } )
{ "collectionsharded" : "dbname.cart", "ok" : 1 }
```

## CHAPTER 6

Content Management Systems

In this chapter, we'll look at how you can use MongoDB as a data storage engine for a content management system (CMS). In particular, we'll examine two main areas of CMS development. Our first use case, "Metadata and Asset Management" (page 101), deals with how we can model our metadata (pages, blog posts, photos, videos) using MongoDB.

Our next use case, "Storing Comments" (page 111), explores several different approaches to storing user comments in a CMS, along with the trade-offs for each approach.

Metadata and Asset Management

In any kind of a content management system, you need to decide on the basic objects that the CMS will be managing. For this section, we've chosen to model our CMS on the popular Drupal (*http://www.drupal.org*) CMS. (Drupal *does* have a MongoDB plug-in, but we've chosen a simpler implementation for the purposes of illustration in this section.) Here, we explore how MongoDB can be used as a natural data model backend for such a CMS, focusing on the storage of the major types of content in a CMS.

Solution Overview

To build this system, we'll use MongoDB's flexible schema to store all content "nodes" in a single collection nodes regardless of type. This guide provides prototype schemas and describes common operations for the following primary node types:

Basic page
> Basic pages are useful for displaying infrequently changing text such as an *About* page. With a basic page, the salient information is the title and the content.

Blog post
> Blog posts are part of a "stream" of posts from users on the CMS, and store title, author, content, and date as relevant information.

Photo
> Photos participate in photo galleries, and store title, description, author, and date along with the actual photo binary data.

Note that each type of node may participate in *groups* of nodes. In particular, a *basic page* would be part of a *folder* on the site, a *blog post* would be part of a *blog*, and a photo would be part of a *gallery*. This section won't go into details about how we might group these nodes together, nor will it address navigational structure.

Schema Design

Although documents in the `nodes` collection contain content of different types, all documents have a similar structure and a set of common fields. Consider the following prototype document for a "basic page" node type:

```
{ _id: ObjectId(...)),
  metadata: {
    nonce: ObjectId(...),
    type: 'basic-page'
    parent_id: ObjectId(...),
    slug: 'about',
    title: 'About Us',
    created: ISODate(...),
    author: { _id: ObjectId(...), name: 'Rick' },
    tags: [ ... ],
    detail: { text: '# About Us\n...' }
  }
}
```

Most fields are descriptively titled. The `parent_id` field identifies groupings of items, as in a photo gallery, or a particular blog. The `slug` field holds a URL-friendly unique representation of the node, usually that is unique within its section for generating URLs.

All documents also have a `detail` field that varies with the document type. For the basic page, the detail field might hold the text of the page. For a blog entry, the `detail` field might hold a subdocument. Consider the following prototype for a blog entry:

```
{ ...
  metadata: {
    ...
    type: 'blog-entry',
    parent_id: ObjectId(...),
    slug: '2012-03-noticed-the-news',
    ...,
    detail: {
      publish_on: ISODate(...),
      text: 'I noticed the news from Washington today...'
    }
  }
}
```

Photos require a different approach. Because photos can be potentially large, it's important to separate the binary photo storage from the node's metadata. GridFS provides the ability to store larger files in MongoDB.

GridFS

GridFS is actually a convention, implemented *in the client*, for storing large blobs of binary data in MongoDB. MongoDB documents are limited in size to (currently) 16 MB. This means that if your blob of data is larger than 16 MB, or *might be* larger than 16 MB, you need to split the data over multiple documents.

This is just what GridFS does. In GridFS, each blob is represented by:

- One document that contains metadata about the blob (filename, md5 checksum, MIME type, etc.), and
- One or more documents containing the actual contents of the blob, broken into 256 kB "chunks."

While GridFS is not optimized in the same way as a traditional distributed filesystem, it is often more convenient to use. In particular, it's convenient to use GridFS:

- For storing large binary objects directly in the database, as in the photo album example, or
- For storing file-like data where you need something *like* a distributed filesystem but you don't want to actually set up a distributed filesystem.

As always, it's best to test with your own data to see if GridFS is a good fit for you.

GridFS stores data in two collections—in this case, `cms.assets.files`, which stores metadata, and `cms.assets.chunks`, which stores the data itself. Consider the following prototype document from the `cms.assets.files` collection:

```
{ _id: ObjectId(…),
  length: 123...,
  chunkSize: 262144,
  uploadDate: ISODate(…),
  contentType: 'image/jpeg',
  md5: 'ba49a...',
  metadata: {
    nonce: ObjectId(…),
    slug: '2012-03-invisible-bicycle',
    type: 'photo',
    locked: ISODate(...),
    parent_id: ObjectId(...),
    title: 'Kitteh',
    created: ISODate(…),
    author: { _id: ObjectId(…), name: 'Jared' },
    tags: [ … ],
```

```
    detail: {
      filename: 'kitteh_invisible_bike.jpg',
      resolution: [ 1600, 1600 ], … }
  }
}
```

Note that in this example, most of our document looks exactly the same as a basic page document. This helps to facilitate querying nodes, allowing us to use the same code for either a photo or a basic page. This is facilitated by the fact that GridFS reserves the `metadata` field for user-defined data.

Operations

This section outlines a number of common operations for building and interacting with the metadata and asset layer of the CMS for all node types. All examples in this document use the Python programming language, but of course you can implement this system using any language you choose.

Create and edit content nodes

The most common operations inside of a CMS center on creating and editing content. Consider the following `insert` operation:

```
db.cms.nodes.insert({
    'metadata': {
        'nonce': ObjectId(),
        'parent_id': ObjectId(...),
        'slug': '2012-03-noticed-the-news',
        'type': 'blog-entry',
        'title': 'Noticed in the News',
        'created': datetime.utcnow(),
        'author': { 'id': user_id, 'name': 'Rick' },
        'tags': [ 'news', 'musings' ],
        'detail': {
            'publish_on': datetime.utcnow(),
            'text': 'I noticed the news from Washington today…' }
    }
})
```

One field that we've used but not yet explained is the nonce field. A **nonce** is a value that is designed to be only used once. In our CMS, we've used a nonce to mark each node when it is inserted or updated. This helps us to detect problems where two users might be modifying the same node simultaneously. Suppose, for example, that Alice and Bob both decide to update the *About* page for their CMS, and the sequence goes something like this (Figure 6-1):

1. Alice saves her changes. The page refreshes, and she sees her new version.

2. Bob then saves *his* changes. The page refreshes, and he sees *his* new version.

3. Alice and Bob both refresh the page. Both of them see Bob's version. Alice's version has been lost, and Bob didn't even know he was overwriting it!

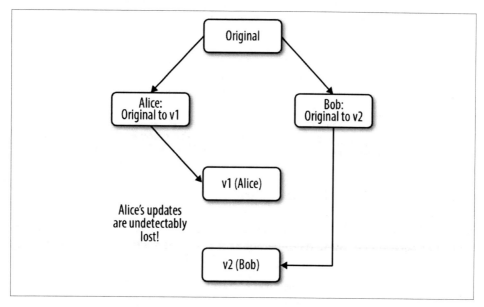

Figure 6-1. Alice and Bob edit collision

A nonce can fix this problem by ensuring that updates to a node only succeed when you're updating the same version of the document that you're editing, as shown in Figure 6-2.

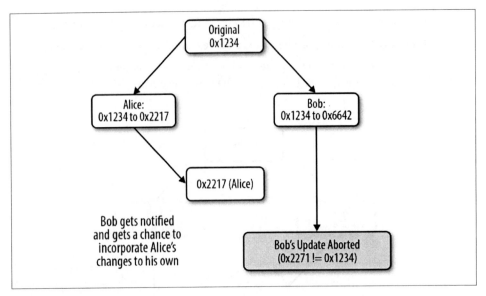

Figure 6-2. Alice and Bob edit collision detected

By using our nonce field, we can detect editing collisions and give the user the opportunity to resolve them. Our update operation for a content node, then, looks something like the following:

```
def update_text(parent_id, slug, nonce, text):
    result = db.cms.nodes.update(
        { 'metadata.parent_id': parent_id,
          'metadata.slug': slug,
          'metadata.nonce': nonce },
        { '$set':{'metadata.detail.text': text,
                  'metadata.nonce': ObjectId() } },
        safe=True) ❶
    if not result['updatedExisting']:
        raise ConflictError() ❷
```

❶   Here, we use safe mode to let MongoDB tell us whether it found a document to update or not. By including the nonce in the query, we ensure that the document will only be updated if it has not been modified since we loaded the nonce (which may have been a different web request).

❷   Here, we simply raise an exception. More advanced approaches might keep a history of the document and show differences, allowing the user to resolve them manually.

We might also want to perform metadata edits to the item such as adding tags:

```
db.cms.nodes.update(
    { 'metadata.parent_id': parent_id, 'metadata.slug': slug },
    { '$addToSet': { 'tags': { '$each': [ 'interesting', 'funny' ] } } })
```

In this example, the $addToSet operator will only add values to the tags field if they do
not already exist in the tags array; there's no need to supply or update the nonce.

To support updates and queries on the metadata.parent_id and metadata.slug fields
and to ensure that two editors don't create two documents with the same parent or slug,
we can create a unique index on these two fields:

```
>>> db.cms.nodes.ensure_index([
...     ('metadata.parent_id', 1), ('metadata.slug', 1)], unique=True)
```

Upload a photo

Uploading photos to our CMS requires some extra attention, as the amount of data to
be transferred can be substantially higher than for a "normal" content node. This led to
our decision to use GridFS for the storage of photos. Furthermore, we would rather *not*
load the entire photo's data into memory at once, so the following code "streams" data
through to MongoDB, one chunk at a time:

```
def upload_new_photo(
    input_file, parent_id, slug, title, author, tags, details):
    fs = GridFS(db, 'cms.assets')
    now = datetime.utcnow()
    with fs.new_file(
        content_type='image/jpeg',  ❶
        metadata=dict(
            nonce=bson.ObjectId(),
            type='photo',
            locked=now,  ❷
            parent_id=parent_id,
            slug=slug,
            title=title,
            created=now,
            author=author,
            tags=tags,
            detail=detail)) as upload_file:
        while True:
            chunk = input_file.read(upload_file.chunk_size)  ❸
            if not chunk: break
            upload_file.write(chunk)
    # unlock the file
    db.assets.files.update(  ❹
        {'_id': upload_file._id},
        {'$set': { 'locked': None } } )
```

❶   Though most of our photo information goes into the metadata field, the MIME
     content type is one of the supported fields at the "top level" of GridFS files.

❷ When creating a photo, we set a locked value to indicate when the upload started. This helps us detect stalled uploads and conflicting updates later.

❸ Since we're storing files in GridFS in chunks of chunk_size, we read them from the client using the same buffer size.

❹ Finally, we unlock the record, signifying that the upload is completed.

Because uploading the photo spans multiple documents and is a nonatomic operation, we "lock" the file during upload by writing the current datetime in the record. The following code shows how the locked field is used to manage updates to the photo content:

```
def update_photo_content(input_file, parent_id, slug):
    fs = GridFS(db, 'cms.assets')

    # Delete the old version if it's unlocked or was locked more than 5
    #     minutes ago
    file_obj = db.cms.assets.find_one(
        { 'metadata.parent_id': parent_id,
          'metadata.slug': slug,
          'metadata.locked': None })
    if file_obj is None:
        threshold = datetime.utcnow() - timedelta(seconds=300)
        file_obj = db.cms.assets.find_one(
            { 'metadata.parent_id': parent_id,
              'metadata.slug': slug,
              'metadata.locked': { '$lt': threshold } })
    if file_obj is None: raise FileDoesNotExist()
    fs.delete(file_obj['_id']) ❶

    # update content, keep metadata unchanged
    file_obj['locked'] = datetime.utcnow()
    with fs.new_file(**file_obj):
        while True:
            chunk = input_file.read(upload_file.chunk_size)
            if not chunk: break
            upload_file.write(chunk)
    # unlock the file
    db.assets.files.update(
        {'_id': upload_file._id},
        {'$set': { 'locked': None } } )
```

❶ Note that we need to invoke the delete method on the GridFS rather than just use our normal remove MongoDB functionality. This is because we need to make sure that both the document in cms.assets.files is removed *and* the corresponding chunks in cms.assets.chunks.

As with the basic operations, editing tags is almost trivial:

```
db.cms.assets.files.update(
    { 'metadata.parent_id': parent_id, 'metadata.slug': slug },
    { '$addToSet': { 'metadata.tags': { '$each': [ 'interesting', 'funny']}}})
```

Since our queries tend to use both `metadata.parent_id` and `metadata.slug`, a unique index on this combination is sufficient to get good performance:

```
>>> db.cms.assets.files.ensure_index([
...     ('metadata.parent_id', 1), ('metadata.slug', 1)], unique=True)
```

Locate and render a node

To locate a "normal" node based on the value of `metadata.parent_id` and `metadata.slug`, we can use the `find_one` operation rather than `find`:

```
node = db.nodes.find_one({'metadata.parent_id': parent_id,
                          'metadata.slug': slug })
```

To locate an image based on the value of `metadata.parent_id` and `metadata.slug`, we use the GridFS method `get_version`:

```
code,sourceCode,python
fs = GridFS(db, 'cms.assets')
with fs.get_version({'metadata.parent_id': parent_id, 'metadata.slug': slug })
  as img_fpo:
    # do something with the image file
```

Search for nodes by tag

To retrieve a list of "normal" nodes based on their tags, the query is straightforward:

```
nodes = db.nodes.find({'metadata.tags': tag })
```

To retrieve a list of images based on their tags, we'll perform a search on `cms.assets.files` directly:

```
image_file_objects = db.cms.assets.files.find({'metadata.tags': tag })
fs = GridFS(db, 'cms.assets')
for image_file_object in db.cms.assets.files.find(
    {'metadata.tags': tag }):
    image_file = fs.get(image_file_object['_id'])
    # do something with the image file
```

In order to make these queries perform well, of course, we need an index on `metadata.tags`:

```
>>> db.cms.nodes.ensure_index('metadata.tags')
>>> db.cms.assets.files.ensure_index('metadata.tags')
```

Generate a feed of recently published blog articles

One common operation in a blog is to find the most recently published blog post, sorted in descending order by date, for use on the index page of the site, or in an RSS or ATOM feed:

```
articles = db.nodes.find({
    'metadata.parent_id': 'my-blog'
    'metadata.published': { '$lt': datetime.utcnow() } })
articles = articles.sort({'metadata.published': -1})
```

Since we're now searching on `parent_id` and `published`, we need an index on these fields:

```
>>> db.cms.nodes.ensure_index(
...     [ ('metadata.parent_id', 1), ('metadata.published', -1) ])
```

Sharding Concerns

In a CMS, read performance is more critical than write performance. To achieve the best read performance in a shard cluster, we need to ensure that mongos can route queries to their particular shards.

 Keep in mind that MongoDB *cannot* enforce unique indexes across shards. There is, however, one exception to this rule. If the unique index is the shard key itself, MongoDB can continue to enforce uniqueness in the index. Since we've been using the compound key (`metadata.par ent_id`, `metadata.slug`) as a unique index, *and we have relied on this index for correctness*, we need to be sure to use it as our shard key.

To shard our node collections, we can use the following commands:

```
>>> db.command('shardcollection', 'dbname.cms.nodes', {
...     key : { 'metadata.parent_id': 1, 'metadata.slug' : 1 } })
{ "collectionsharded": "dbname.cms.nodes", "ok": 1}
>>> db.command('shardcollection', 'dbname.cms.assets.files', {
...     key : { 'metadata.parent_id': 1, 'metadata.slug' : 1 } })
{ "collectionsharded": "dbname.cms.assets.files", "ok": 1}
```

To shard the `cms.assets.chunks` collection, we need to use the `files_id` field as the shard key. The following operation will shard the collection (note that we have appended the `_id` field to guard against an *enormous* photo being unsplittable across chunks):

```
>>> db.command('shardcollection', 'dbname.cms.assets.chunks', {
...     key : { 'files_id': 1, '_id': 1 } })
{ "collectionsharded": "dbname.cms.assets.chunks", "ok": 1}
```

Note that sharding on the _id field ensures routable queries because all reads from GridFS must first look up the document in `cms.assets.files` and then look up the chunks separately by `files_id`.

Storing Comments

Most content management systems include the ability to store and display user-submitted comments along with any of the normal content nodes. This section outlines the basic patterns for storing user-submitted comments in such a CMS.

Solution Overview

MongoDB provides a number of different approaches for storing data like user comments on content from a CMS. There is no one correct implementation, but rather a number of common approaches and known considerations for each approach. This section explores the implementation details and trade-offs of each option. The three basic patterns are:

Store each comment in its own document
> This approach provides the greatest flexibility at the expense of some additional application-level complexity. For instance, in a comment-per-document approach, it is possible to display comments in either chronological or threaded order. Furthermore, it is not necessary in this approach to place any arbitrary limit on the number of comments that can be attached to a particular object.

Embed all comments in the "parent" document
> This approach provides the greatest possible performance for displaying comments at the expense of flexibility: the structure of the comments in the document controls the display format. (You can, of course, re-sort the comments on the client side, but this requires extra work on the application side.) The number of comments, however, is strictly limited by MongoDB's document size limit.

Store comments separately from the "parent," but grouped together with each other
> This hybrid design provides more flexibility than the pure embedding approach, but provides almost the same performance.

Also consider that comments can be *threaded*, where comments are always replies to a "parent" item or to another comment, which carries certain architectural requirements discussed next.

Approach: One Document per Comment

If we wish to store each comment in its own document, the documents in our `comments` collection would have the following structure:

```
{
    _id: ObjectId(...),
    node_id: ObjectId(...),
    slug: '34db',
    posted: ISODateTime(...),
    author: {
            id: ObjectId(...),
            name: 'Rick'
         },
    text: 'This is so bogus ... '
}
```

This form is only suitable for displaying comments in chronological order. Comments store the following:

- The `node_id` field that references the node parent
- A URL-compatible `slug` identifier
- A `posted` timestamp
- An `author` subdocument that contains a reference to a user's profile in the `id` field and their name in the `name` field
- The full `text` of the comment

In order to support threaded comments, we need to use a slightly different structure:

```
{
    _id: ObjectId(...),
    node_id: ObjectId(...),
    parent_id: ObjectId(...),
    slug: '34db/8bda'
    full_slug: '2012.02.08.12.21.08:34db/2012.02.09.22.19.16:8bda',
    posted: ISODateTime(...),
    author: {
            id: ObjectId(...),
            name: 'Rick'
         },
    text: 'This is so bogus ... '
}
```

This structure:

- Adds a `parent_id` field that stores the contents of the `_id` field of the parent comment
- Modifies the `slug` field to hold a path composed of the parent or parent's slug and this comment's unique slug
- Adds a `full_slug` field that combines the slugs and time information to make it easier to sort documents in a threaded discussion by date

Operation: Post a new comment

To post a new comment in a chronologically ordered (i.e., without discussion threading) system, we just need to use a regular `insert()`:

```
slug = generate_pseudorandom_slug()
db.comments.insert({
    'node_id': node_id,
    'slug': slug,
    'posted': datetime.utcnow(),
    'author': author_info,
    'text': comment_text })
```

To insert a comment for a system with threaded comments, we first need to generate the appropriate `slug` and `full_slug` values based on the parent comment:

```
posted = datetime.utcnow()

# generate the unique portions of the slug and full_slug
slug_part = generate_pseudorandom_slug()
full_slug_part = posted.strftime('%Y.%m.%d.%H.%M.%S') + ':' + slug_part
# load the parent comment (if any)
if parent_slug:
    parent = db.comments.find_one(
        {'node_id': node_id, 'slug': parent_slug })
    slug = parent['slug'] + '/' + slug_part
    full_slug = parent['full_slug'] + '/' + full_slug_part
else:
    slug = slug_part
    full_slug = full_slug_part

# actually insert the comment
db.comments.insert({
    'node_id': node_id,
    'slug': slug,
    'full_slug': full_slug,
    'posted': posted,
    'author': author_info,
    'text': comment_text })
```

Operation: View paginated comments

To view comments that are not threaded, we just need to select all comments participating in a discussion and sort by the `posted` field. For example:

```
cursor = db.comments.find({'node_id': node_id})
cursor = cursor.sort('posted')
cursor = cursor.skip(page_num * page_size)
cursor = cursor.limit(page_size)
```

Since the `full_slug` field contains both hierarchical information (via the path) and chronological information, we can use a simple sort on the `full_slug` field to retrieve a threaded view:

```
cursor = db.comments.find({'node_id': node_id})
cursor = cursor.sort('full_slug')
cursor = cursor.skip(page_num * page_size)
cursor = cursor.limit(page_size)
```

To support these queries efficiently, maintain two compound indexes on `node_id, posted` and `node_id, full_slug`:

```
>>> db.comments.ensure_index([
...     ('node_id', 1), ('posted', 1)])
>>> db.comments.ensure_index([
...     ('node_id', 1), ('full_slug', 1)])
```

Operation: Retrieve comments via direct links

To directly retrieve a comment, without needing to page through all comments, we can select by the `slug` field:

```
comment = db.comments.find_one({
    'node_id': node_id,
    'slug': comment_slug})
```

We can also retrieve a "subdiscussion," or a comment and all of its descendants recursively, by performing a regular expression prefix query on the `full_slug` field:

```
import re

subdiscussion = db.comments.find_one({
    'node_id': node_id,
    'full_slug': re.compile('^' + re.escape(parent_full_slug)) })
subdiscussion = subdiscussion.sort('full_slug')
```

Since we've already created indexes on { `node_id: 1, full_slug: 1` } to support retrieving subdiscussions, we don't need to add any other indexes here to achieve good performance.

Approach: Embedding All Comments

This design embeds the entire discussion of a comment thread inside of its parent node document.

Consider the following prototype `topic` document:

```
{ _id: ObjectId(...),
  ...,
  metadata: {
    ...
    comments: [
```

```
    { posted: ISODateTime(...),
      author: { id: ObjectId(...), name: 'Rick' },
      text: 'This is so bogus ... ' },
    ... ],
  }
}
```

This structure is only suitable for a chronological display of all comments because it embeds comments in chronological order. Each document in the array in the com ments contains the comment's date, author, and text.

To support threading using this design, we would need to embed comments within comments, using a structure more like the following:

```
{ _id: ObjectId(...),
  ... lots of topic data ...
  metadata: {
    ...,
    replies: [
      { posted: ISODateTime(...),
        author: { id: ObjectId(...), name: 'Rick' },
        text: 'This is so bogus ... ',
        replies: [
            { author: { ... }, ... },
            ... ]
      }
      ... ]
  }
}
```

Here, the replies field in each comment holds the subcomments, which can in turn hold subcomments.

Operation: Post a new comment

To post a new comment in a chronologically ordered (i.e., unthreaded) system, we need the following update:

```
db.cms.nodes.update(
    { ... node specification ... },
    { '$push': { 'metadata.comments': {
        'posted': datetime.utcnow(),
        'author': author_info,
        'text': comment_text } } } )
```

The $push operator inserts comments into the comments array in correct chronological order. For threaded discussions, the update operation is more complex. To reply to a comment, the following code assumes that it can retrieve the *path* as a list of positions, for the parent comment:

```
if path != []:
    str_path = '.'.join('replies.%d' % part for part in path)
```

```
        str_path += '.replies'
    else:
        str_path = 'replies'
    db.cms.nodes.update(
        { ... node specification ... },
        { '$push': {
            'metadata.' + str_path: {
                'posted': datetime.utcnow(),
                'author': author_info,
                'text': comment_text } } } )
```

This constructs a field name of the form `metadata.replies.0.replies.2...` as `str_path` and then uses this value with the `$push` operator to insert the new comment into the `replies` array.

Operation: View paginated comments

To view the comments in a nonthreaded design, we need to use the `$slice` operator:

```
node = db.cms.nodes.find_one(
    { ... node specification ... },
    { ... some fields relevant to your page from the root discussion ...,
      'metadata.comments': { '$slice': [ page_num * page_size, page_size ] }
    })
```

To return paginated comments for the threaded design, we must retrieve the whole document and paginate the comments within the application:

```
node = db.cms.nodes.find_one(... node specification ...)

def iter_comments(obj):
    for reply in obj['replies']:
        yield reply
        for subreply in iter_comments(reply):
            yield subreply

paginated_comments = itertools.slice(
    iter_comments(node),
    page_size * page_num,
    page_size * (page_num + 1))
```

Operation: Retrieve a comment via direct links

Instead of retrieving comments via slugs as in "Approach: One Document per Comment" (page 111), the following example retrieves comments using their position in the comment list or tree. For chronological (i.e., nonthreaded) comments, we'll just use the `$slice` operator to extract a single comment, as follows:

```
node = db.cms.nodes.find_one(
    {'node_id': node_id},
    {'comments': { '$slice': [ position, position ] } })
comment = node['comments'][0]
```

For threaded comments, we must know the correct path through the tree in our application, as follows:

```
node = db.cms.nodes.find_one(... node specification ...)
current = node.metadata
for part in path:
    current = current.replies[part]
comment = current
```

Approach: Hybrid Schema Design

In the "hybrid approach," we store comments in "buckets" that hold about 100 comments. Consider the following example document:

```
{ _id: ObjectId(...),
  node_id: ObjectId(...),
  page: 1,
  count: 42,
  comments: [ {
        slug: '34db',
        posted: ISODateTime(...),
        author: { id: ObjectId(...), name: 'Rick' },
        text: 'This is so bogus ... ' },
     ... ]
}
```

Each document maintains page and count data that contains metadata regarding the page number and the comment count in this page, in addition to the comments array that holds the comments themselves.

Operation: Post a new comment

In order to post a new comment, we need to $push the comment onto the last page and $inc that page's comment count. Consider the following example that adds a comment onto the last page of comments for some node:

```
def post_comment(node, comment):
    result = db.comment_pages.update(
        { 'node_id': node['_id'],
          'page': node['num_comment_pages'],
          'count': { '$lt': 100 } }, ❶
        { '$inc': { 'count': 1 },
          '$push': { 'comments': comment } },
        upsert=True)

    if not result['updatedExisting']:
        db.cms.nodes.update(
            { '_id': node['_id'],
              'num_comment_pages': node['num_comment_pages'] },
            { '$inc': { 'num_comment_pages': 1 } }) ❷
        db.comment_pages.update(
```

```
                { 'node_id': node['_id'],
                  'page': node['num_comment_pages'] + 1},
                { '$inc': { 'count': 1 },
                  '$push': { 'comments': comment } },
                upsert=True) ❸
```

There are a few things to note about this code:

❶   The first update will only $push a comment if the page is not yet full.

❷   If the last comment page *is* full, we need to increment the num_comment_pages property in the node (so long as some other process has not already incremented that property).

❸   We also need to re-run the update to $push the comment onto the newly created comment page. Here, we've dropped the count constraint to make sure the $push goes through. (While it's technically possible that 100 other concurrent writers were adding comments and the new page is already full, it's highly unlikely, and the application works just fine if there happen to be 101 comments on a page.)

To support the update operations, we need to maintain a compound index on node_id, page in the comment_pages collection:

```
>>> db.comment_pages.ensure_index([
...     ('node_id', 1), ('page', 1)])
```

Operation: View paginated comments

The following function defines how to paginate comments where the number of comments on a page is not known precisely (i.e., with *roughly* 100 comments, as in this case):

```
def find_comments(discussion_id, skip, limit):
    query = db.comment_pages.find(
        { 'node_id': node_id } )
    query = query.sort('page')
    for page in query:
        new_skip = skip - page['count']
        if new_skip >= 0:
            skip = new_skip
            continue
        elif skip > 0:
            comments = page['comments'][skip:]
        else:
            comments = page['comments']
        skip = new_skip
        for comment in comments:
            if limit == 0:
                break
            limit -= 1
            yield comment
        if limit == 0: break
```

Here, we iterate through the pages until our `skip` requirement is satisfied, then `yield` comments until our `limit` requirement is satisfied. For example, if we have three pages of comments with 100, 102, 101, and 22 comments on each page, and we wish to retrieve comments where `skip=300` and `limit=50`, we'd use the following algorithm:

Skip	Limit	Discussion
300	50	Page 0 has 100 comments, so `skip -= 100`.
200	50	Page 1 has 102 comments, so `skip -= 102`.
98	50	Page 2 has 101 comments, so set `skip=0` and return last 3 comments.
0	47	Page 3 has 22 comments, so return them all and set `limit-= 22`.
0	25	There are no more pages; terminate loop.

Operation: Retrieve a comment via direct links

To retrieve a comment directly without paging through all preceding pages of commentary, we'll use the slug to find the correct page, and then use application logic to find the correct comment:

```
page = db.comment_pages.find_one(
    { 'node_id': node_id,
      'comments.slug': comment_slug},
    { 'comments': 1 })
for comment in page['comments']:
    if comment['slug'] = comment_slug:
        break
```

To perform this query efficiently, we'll need a new index on `node_id, comments.slug` (this is assuming that slugs are only guaranteed unique *within* a node):

```
>>> db.comment_pages.ensure_index([
...     ('node_id', 1), ('comments.slug', 1)])
```

Sharding Concerns

For all of the architectures just discussed, we will want the `node_id` field to participate in any shard key we pick.

For applications that use the "one document per comment" approach, we'll use the `slug` (or `full_slug`, in the case of threaded comments) fields in the shard key to allow the `mongos` instances to route requests by `slug`:

```
>>> db.command('shardcollection', 'dbname.comments', {
...     'key' : { 'node_id' : 1, 'slug': 1 } })
{ "collectionsharded" : "dbname.comments", "ok" : 1 }
```

In the case of comments that are fully embedded in parent content, the comments will just participate in the sharding of their parent document.

For hybrid documents, we can use the page number of the comment page in the shard key along with the `node_id` to prevent a single discussion from creating a giant, unsplittable chunk of comments. The appropriate command for this is as follows:

```
>>> db.command('shardcollection', 'dbname.comment_pages', {
...     key : { 'node_id' : 1, 'page': 1 } })
{ "collectionsharded" : "dbname.comment_pages", "ok" : 1 }
```

## CHAPTER 7

Online Advertising Networks

In this chapter, we'll examine building an online advertising network that connects advertisers and media websites. Advertisers provide the ads for display, with each ad designed for a particular *ad zone*. Media sites, on the other hand, provide content pages for display with various regions marked for serving ads. When the media site displays a page, it makes a request to the ad network for one or more ads to display in its ad zones.

As part of the ad serving, the ad network records the number of pageviews of each ad in order to track statistics for the ad, which may then also be used to bill the advertiser.

Solution Overview

This solution is structured as a progressive refinement of the ad network, starting out with the basic data storage requirements and adding more advanced features to the schema to support more advanced ad targeting. The key performance criterion for this solution is the latency between receiving an ad request and returning the (targeted) ad to be displayed.

Design 1: Basic Ad Serving

A basic ad-serving algorithm consists of the following steps:

1. The network receives a request for an ad, specifying at a minimum the site_id and zone_id to be served.

2. The network consults its inventory of ads available to display and chooses an ad based on various business rules.

3. The network returns the actual ad to be displayed, recording the pageview for the ad as well.

This design uses the `site_id` and `zone_id` submitted with the ad request, as well as information stored in the ad inventory collection, to make the ad targeting decisions. Later examples will build on this, allowing more advanced ad targeting.

Schema Design

A very basic schema for storing ads available to be served consists of a single collection, `ad.zone`:

```
{
  _id: ObjectId(...),
  site_id: 'cnn',
  zone_id: 'banner',
  ads: [
    { campaign_id: 'mercedes:c201204_sclass_4',
      ad_unit_id: 'banner23a',
      ecpm: 250 },
    { campaign_id: 'mercedes:c201204_sclass_4',
      ad_unit_id: 'banner23b',
      ecpm: 250 },
    { campaign_id: 'bmw:c201204_eclass_1',
      ad_unit_id: 'banner12',
      ecpm: 200 },
    ... ]
}
```

Note that for each site-zone combination you'll be storing a list of ads, sorted by their *eCPM* values.

eCPM, CPM, CPC, CTR, etc.

The world of online advertising is full of somewhat cryptic acronyms. Most of the decisions made by the ad network in this chapter will be based on the eCPM, or effective cost per mille. This is a synthetic measure meant to allow comparison between *CPM* (cost per mille) ads, which are priced based on the number of impressions, and *CPC* (cost per click) ads, which are priced per click.

The eCPM of a CPM ad is just the CPM. Calculating the eCPM of a CPC ad is fairly straightforward, based on the *CTR* (click-through rate), which is defined as the number of clicks per ad impression. The formula for eCPM for a CPC ad then is:

$eCPM = CPC \times CTR \times 1000$

In this chapter, we'll assume that the eCPM is already known for each ad, though you'll obviously need to calculate it in a real ad network.

Operation: Choose an Ad to Serve

The query we'll use to choose which ad to serve selects a compatible ad and sorts by the advertiser's ecpm bid in order to maximize the ad network's profits:

```python
from itertools import groupby
from random import choice

def choose_ad(site_id, zone_id):
    site = db.ad.zone.find_one({
        'site_id': site_id, 'zone_id': zone_id}) ❶
    if site is None: return None
    if len(site['ads']) == 0: return None
    ecpm_groups = groupby(site['ads'], key=lambda ad:ad['ecpm']) ❷
    ecpm, ad_group = ecpm_groups.next()
    return choice(list(ad_group))❸
```

❶ First, we find a compatible site and zone for the ad request.

❷ Next, we group the ads based on their eCPM. This step requires that the ads already be sorted by descending eCPM.

❸ Finally, we randomly select an ad from the most expensive ad group.

In order to execute the ad choice with the lowest latency possible, we need to maintain a compound index on site_id, zone_id:

```python
>>> db.ad.zone.ensure_index([
...     ('site_id', 1),
...     ('zone_id', 1) ])
```

Operation: Make an Ad Campaign Inactive

One case we need to deal with is making a campaign inactive. This may happen for a variety of reasons. For instance, the campaign may have reached its end date or exhausted its budget for the current time period. In this case, the logic is fairly straightforward:

```python
def deactivate_campaign(campaign_id):
    db.ad.zone.update(
        { 'ads.campaign_id': campaign_id },
        {' $pull': { 'ads', { 'campaign_id': campaign_id } } },
        multi=True)
```

This update statement first selects only those ad zones that had available ads from the given campaign_id and then uses the $pull modifier to remove them from rotation.

To execute the multiupdate quickly, we'll keep an index on the ads.campaign_id field:

```python
>>> db.ad.zone.ensure_index('ads.campaign_id')
```

Sharding Concerns

In order to scale beyond the capacity of a single replica set, you will need to shard the
ad.zone collection. To maintain the lowest possible latency (and the highest possible
throughput) in the ad selection operation, the shard key needs to be chosen to allow
MongoDB to route the ad.zone query to a single shard. In this case, a good approach
is to shard on the site_id, zone_id combination:

```
>>> db.command('shardcollection', 'dbname.ads.ad.zone', {
...     'key': {'site_id': 1, 'zone_id': 1} })
{ "collectionsharded": "dbname.ads.ad.zone", "ok": 1 }
```

Design 2: Adding Frequency Capping

One problem with the logic described in "Design 1: Basic Ad Serving" (page 121) is that
it will tend to display the same ad over and over again until the campaign's budget is
exhausted. To mitigate this, advertisers may wish to limit the frequency with which a
given user is presented a particular ad. This process is called frequency capping and is
an example of user profile targeting in advertising.

In order to perform frequency capping (or any type of user targeting), the ad network
needs to maintain a profile for each visitor, typically implemented as a cookie in the
user's browser. This cookie, effectively a user_id, is then transmitted to the ad network
when logging impressions, clicks, conversions, etc., as well as the ad-serving decision.
This section focuses on how that profile data impacts the ad-serving decision.

Schema Design

In order to use the user profile data, we need to store it. In this case, it's stored in a
collection ad.user:

```
{
  _id: 'cookie_value',
  advertisers: {
    mercedes: {
      impressions: [
        { date: ISODateTime(...),
          campaign: 'c201204_sclass_4',
          ad_unit_id: 'banner23a',
          site_id: 'cnn',
          zone_id: 'banner' } },
        ... ],
      clicks: [
        { date: ISODateTime(...),
          campaign: 'c201204_sclass_4',
          ad_unit_id: 'banner23a',
          site_id: 'cnn',
          zone_id: 'banner' } },
```

```
      ... ],
    bmw: [ ... ],
      ...
  }
}
```

There are a few things to note about the user profile:

- All data is embedded in a single profile document. When you need to query this data (detailed next), you don't necessarily know which advertiser's ads you'll be showing, so it's a good practice to embed all advertisers in a single document.

- The event information is grouped by event type within an advertiser, and sorted by timestamp. This allows rapid lookups of a stream of a particular type of event.

Operation: Choose an Ad to Serve

The query we'll use to choose which ad to serve now needs to iterate through ads in order of profitability and select the "best" ad that also satisfies the advertiser's targeting rules (in this case, the frequency cap):

```python
from itertools import groupby
from random import shuffle
from datetime import datetime, timedelta

def choose_ad(site_id, zone_id, user_id):
    site = db.ad.zone.find_one({
        'site_id': site_id, 'zone_id': zone_id}) ❶
    if site is None or len(site['ads']) == 0: return None
    ads = ad_iterator(site['ads']) ❷
    user = db.ad.user.find_one({'user_id': user_id}) ❸
    if user is None:
        # any ad is acceptable for an unknown user
        return ads.next()
    for ad in ads: ❹
        advertiser_id = ad['campaign_id'].split(':', 1)[0]
        if ad_is_acceptable(ad, user[advertiser_id]):
            return ad
    return None
```

❶ Here we once again find all ads that are targeted to that particular site and ad zone.

❷ Next, we have factored out a Python generator that will iterate through all the ads in order of profitability.

❸ Now we load the user profile for the given user. If there is no profile, we return the first ad in the iterator.

❹ Finally, we iterate through each of the ads and check it using the `ad_is_accept able` function.

Here's our `ad_iterator` generator:

```
def ad_iterator(ads):
    '''Find available ads, sorted by ecpm, with random sort for ties'''
    ecpm_groups = groupby(ads, key=lambda ad:ad['ecpm'])
    for ecpm, ad_group in ecpm_groups:
        ad_group = list(ad_group)
        shuffle(ad_group)
        for ad in ad_group: yield ad
```

This generator yields the ads in an order that both maximizes profitability and randomly shuffles ads of the same eCPM. Finally, here's our ad filter `ad_is_acceptable`:

```
def ad_is_acceptable(ad, profile):
    '''Returns False if the user has seen the ad today'''
    threshold = datetime.utcnow() - timedelta(days=1)
    for event in reversed(profile['impressions']):
        if event['timestamp'] < threshold: break
        if event['detail']['ad_unit_id'] == ad['ad_unit_id']:
            return False
    return True
```

This function examines all the user's ad impressions for the current day and rejects an ad that has been displayed to that user.

In order to retrieve the user profile with the lowest latency possible, there needs to be an index on the `_id` field, which MongoDB supplies by default.

Sharding

When sharding the `ad.user` collection, choosing the `_id` field as a shard key allows MongoDB to route queries and updates to the user profile:

```
>>> db.command('shardcollection', 'dbname.ads.ad.user', {
...     'key': {'_id': 1 } })
{ "collectionsharded": "dbname.ads.ad.user", "ok": 1 }
```

Design 3: Keyword Targeting

Where frequency capping in the previous section is an example of user profile targeting, you may also wish to perform content targeting so that the user receives relevant ads for the particular page being viewed. The simplest example of this is targeting ads at the result of a search query. In this case, a list of `keywords` is sent to the `choose_ad()` call along with the `site_id`, `zone_id`, and `user_id`.

Schema Design

In order to choose relevant ads, we'll need to expand the ad.zone collection to store relevant keywords for each ad:

```
{
  _id: ObjectId(...),
  site_id: 'cnn',
  zone_id: 'search',
  ads: [
    { campaign_id: 'mercedes:c201204_sclass_4',
      ad_unit_id: 'search1',
      keywords: [ 'car', 'luxury', 'style' ],
      ecpm: 250 },
    { campaign_id: 'mercedes:c201204_sclass_4',
      ad_unit_id: 'search2',
      keywords: [ 'car', 'luxury', 'style' ],
      ecpm: 250 },
    { campaign_id: 'bmw:c201204_eclass_1',
      ad_unit_id: 'search1',
      keywords: [ 'car', 'performance' ],
      ecpm: 200 },
    ... ]
}
```

Operation: Choose a Group of Ads to Serve

In the approach described here, we'll choose a number of ads that match the keywords used in the search, so the following code has been tweaked to return an iterator over ads in descending order of preference. We've also modified the ad_iterator to take the list of keywords as a second parameter:

```
def choose_ads(site_id, zone_id, user_id, keywords):
    site = db.ad.zone.find_one({
        'site_id': site_id, 'zone_id': zone_id})
    if site is None: return []
    ads = ad_iterator(site['ads'], keywords)
    user = db.ad.user.find_one({'user_id': user_id})
    if user is None: return ads
    for ad in ads:
        advertiser_id = ad['campaign_id'].split(':', 1)[0]
        if ad_is_acceptable(ad, user[advertiser_id]):
            yield ad
    return None
```

Our ad_iterator method has been modified to allow us to score ads based on both their eCPM as well as their relevance:

```
def ad_iterator(ads, keywords):
    '''Find available ads, sorted by score, with random sort for ties'''
    keywords = set(keywords)
    scored_ads = [
```

```
        (ad_score(ad, keywords), ad) for ad in ads ]
    score_groups = groupby(
        sorted(scored_ads), key=lambda score, ad: score)
    for score, ad_group in score_groups:
        ad_group = list(ad_group)
        shuffle(ad_group)
        for ad in ad_group: yield ad

def ad_score(ad, keywords):
    '''Compute a desirability score based on the ad eCPM and keywords'''
    matching = set(ad['keywords']).intersection(keywords) return
    ad['ecpm'] * math.log( 1.1 + len(matching))

def ad_is_acceptible(ad, profile):
    # same as above
```

The main thing to note in the preceding code is that ads must now be sorted according to some score, which in this case is computed based on a combination of the ecpm of the ad as well as the number of keywords matched. More advanced use cases may boost the importance of various keywords, but this goes beyond the scope of this use case. One thing to keep in mind is that because the ads are now being sorted at display time, there may be performance issues if a large number of ads are competing for the same display slot.

## CHAPTER 8

Social Networking

In this chapter, we'll explore how you could use MongoDB to store the social graph for a social networking site. We'll look at storing and grouping followers as well as how to publish events to different followers with different privacy settings.

Solution Overview

Our solution assumes a *directed* social graph where a user can choose whether or not to follow another user. Additionally, the user can designate "circles" of users with which to share updates, in order to facilitate fine-grained control of privacy. The solution presented here is designed in such a way as to minimize the number of documents that must be loaded in order to display any given page, even at the expense of complicating updates.

The particulars of what type of data we want to host on a social network obviously depend on the type of social network we're designing, and is largely beyond the scope of this use case. In particular, the main variables that you would have to consider in adapting this use case to your particular situation are:

What data should be in a user profile?
> This may include gender, age, interests, relationship status, and so on for a "personal" social network, or may include resume-type data for a more "business-oriented" social network.

What type of updates are allowed?
> Again, depending on what flavor of social network you are designing, you may wish to allow posts such as status updates, photos, links, check-ins, and polls, or you may wish to restrict your users to links and status updates.

Schema Design

In the solution presented here, we'll use two main "independent" collections and three "dependent" collections to store user profile data and posts.

Independent Collections

The first collection, `social.user`, stores the social graph information for a given user along with the user's profile data:

```
{
  _id: 'T4Y...AC', // base64-encoded ObjectId
  name: 'Rick',
  profile: { ... age, location, interests, etc. ... },
  followers: {
    "T4Y...AD": { name: 'Jared', circles: [ 'python', 'authors'] },
    "T4Y...AF": { name: 'Bernie', circles: [ 'python' ] },
    "T4Y...AI": { name: 'Meghan', circles: [ 'python', 'speakers' ] },
    ...
  ],
  circles: {
    "10gen": {
      "T4Y...AD": { name: 'Jared' },
      "T4Y...AE": { name: 'Max' },
      "T4Y...AF": { name: 'Bernie' },
      "T4Y...AH": { name: 'Paul' },
      ... },
    ...}
4 },
  blocked: ['gh1...0d']
}
```

There are a few things to note about this schema:

- Rather than using a "raw" ObjectId for the _id field, we'll use a base64-encoded version. Although we *can* use raw ObjectId values as keys, we can't use them to "reach inside" a document in a query or an update. By base64-encoding the _id values, we can use queries or updates that include the _id value like circles. 10gen.T4Y...AD.

- We're storing the social graph bidirectionally in the followers and circles collections. While this is technically redundant, having the bidirectional connections is useful both for displaying the user's followers on the profile page, as well as propagating posts to other users, as we'll see later.

- In addition to the normal "positive" social graph, this schema above stores a block list that contains an array of user IDs for posters whose posts never appear on the user's wall or news feed.

- The particular profile data stored for the user is isolated into the `profile` subdocument, allowing us to evolve the profile's schema as necessary without worrying about name collisions with other parts of the schema that need to remain fixed for social graph operations.

Of course, to make the network interesting, it's necessary to add various types of posts. We'll put these in the `social.post` collection:

```
{
    _id: ObjectId(...),
    by: { id: "T4Y...AE", name: 'Max' },
    circles: [ '*public*' ],
    type: 'status',
    ts: ISODateTime(...),
    detail: {
        text: 'Loving MongoDB' },
    comments: [
        { by: { id:"T4Y...AG", name: 'Dwight' },
          ts: ISODateTime(...),
          text: 'Right on!' },
        ... all comments listed ... ]
}
```

Here, the post stores minimal author information (`by`), the post `type`, a timestamp `ts`, post details `detail` (which vary by post type), and a `comments` array. In this case, the schema embeds all comments on a post as a time-sorted flat array. For a more in-depth exploration of the other approaches to storing comments, refer back to "Storing Comments" (page 111).

A couple of points are worthy of further discussion:

- Author information is truncated; just enough is stored in each by property to display the author name and a link to the author profile. If a user wants more detail on a particular author, we can fetch this information as they request it. Storing minimal information like this helps keep the document small (and therefore fast.)

- The visibility of the post is controlled via the `circles` property; any user that is part of one of the listed circles can view the post. The special values `*public*` and `*circles*` allow the user to share a post with the whole world or with any users in any of the posting user's circles, respectively.

- Different types of posts may contain different types of data in the `detail` field. Isolating this polymorphic information into a subdocument is a good practice, helping to identify which parts of the document are common to all posts and which can vary. In this case, we would store different data for a photo post versus a status update, while still keeping the metadata (`_id`, `by`, `circles`, `type`, `ts`, and `com ments`) the same.

Dependent Collections

In addition to independent collections, for optimal performance we'll need to create a few dependent collections that will be used to cache information for display. The first of these collections is the social.wall collection, and is intended to display a "wall" containing posts created by or directed to a particular user. The format of the social.wall collection follows:

```
{
    _id: ObjectId(...),
    user_id: "T4Y...AE",
    month: '201204',
    posts: [
      { id: ObjectId(...),
        ts: ISODateTime(...),
        by: { id: "T4Y...AE", name: 'Max' },
        circles: [ '*public*' ],
        type: 'status',
        detail: { text: 'Loving MongoDB' },
        comments_shown: 3,
        comments: [
          { by: { id: "T4Y...AG", name: 'Dwight',
            ts: ISODateTime(...),
            text: 'Right on!' },
          ... only last 3 comments listed ...
            ]
      },
      { id: ObjectId(...),s
        ts: ISODateTime(...),
        by: { id: "T4Y...AE", name: 'Max' },
        circles: [ '*circles*' ],
        type: 'checkin',
        detail: {
          text: 'Great office!',
          geo: [ 40.724348,-73.997308 ],
          name: '10gen Office',
          photo: 'http://....' },
        comments_shown: 1,
        comments: [
          { by: { id: "T4Y...AD", name: 'Jared' },
            ts: ISODateTime(...),
            text: 'Wrong coast!' },
          ... only last 1 comment listed ...
            ]
      },
      { id: ObjectId(...),
        ts: ISODateTime(...),
        by: { id: "T4Y...g9", name: 'Rick' },
        circles: [ '10gen' ],
        type: 'status',
        detail: {
```

```
          text: 'So when do you crush Oracle?' },
        comments_shown: 2,
        comments: [
          { by: { id: "T4Y...AE", name: 'Max' },
            ts: ISODateTime(...),
            text: 'Soon... ;-)' },
          ... only last 2 comments listed ...
          ]
      },
      ...
    ]
  }
```

There are a few things to note about this schema:

- Each post is listed with an abbreviated number of comments (three might be typical). This is to keep the size of the document reasonable. If we need to display more comments on a post, we'd perform a secondary query on the social.post collection for full details.

- There are actually multiple social.wall documents for each social.user document, one wall document per month. This allows the system to keep a "page" of recent posts in the initial page view, fetching older months if requested.

- Once again, the by properties store only the minimal author information for display, helping to keep this document small.

- The number of comments on each post is stored to allow later updates to find posts with more than a certain number of comments since the $size query operator does not allow inequality comparisons.

The other dependent collection we'll use is social.news, posts from people the user follows. This schema includes much of the same information as the social.wall information, so this document has been abbreviated for clarity:

```
{
  _id: ObjectId(...),
  user_id: "T4Y...AE",
  month: '201204',
  posts: [ ... ]
}
```

Operations

Since these schemas optimize for read performance at the possible expense of write performance, a production system should provide a queueing system for processing updates that may take longer than the desired web request latency.

Viewing a News Feed or Wall Posts

The most common operation on a social network is probably the display of a particular user's news feed, followed by a user's wall posts. Because the `social.news` and `social.wall` collections are optimized for these operations, the query is fairly straightforward. Since these two collections share a schema, viewing the posts for a news feed or a wall are actually quite similar operations, and can be supported by the same code:

```python
def get_posts(collection, user_id, month=None):
    spec = { 'user_id': viewed_user_id }
    if month is not None:
        spec['month'] = {'$lte': month}
    cur = collection.find(spec)
    cur = cur.sort('month', -1)
    for page in cur:
        for post in reversed(page['posts']):
            yield page['month'], post
```

The function `get_posts` will retrieve all the posts on a particular user's wall or news feed in reverse-chronological order. Some special handling is required to efficiently achieve the reverse-chronological ordering:

- The `posts` within a month are actually stored in chronological order, so the order of these posts must be reversed before displaying.

- As a user pages through her wall, it's preferable to avoid fetching the first few months from the server each time. To achieve this, the preceding code specifies the first month to fetch in the `month` argument, passing this in as an `$lte` expression in the query. This can be substantially faster than using a `.skip()` argument to our `.find()`.

- Rather than only yielding the post itself, the post's month is also yielded from the generator. This provides the `month` argument to be used in any subsequent calls to `get_posts`.

There is one other issue that needs to be considered in selecting posts for display: filtering posts for display. In order to choose posts for display, we'll need to use some filter functions on the posts generated by `get_posts`. The first of these filters is used to determine whether to show a post when the user is viewing his or her own wall:

```python
def visible_on_own_wall(user, post):
    '''if poster is followed by user, post is visible'''
    for circle, users in user['circles'].items():
        if post['by']['id'] in users: return True
    return False
```

In addition to the user's wall, our social network provides an "incoming" page that contains all posts directed toward a user regardless of whether that poster is followed by the user. In this case, we need to use the block list to filter posts:

```
def visible_on_own_incoming(user, post):
    '''if poster is not blocked by user, post is visible'''
    return post['by']['id'] not in user['blocked']
```

When viewing a news feed or another user's wall, the permission check is a bit different based on the post's circles property:

```
def visible_post(user, post):
    if post['circles'] == ['*public*']:
        # public posts always visible
        return True
    circles_user_is_in = set(
        user['followers'].get(post['by']['id'], []))
    if not circles_user_is_in:
        # user is not circled by poster; post is invisible
        return False
    if post['circles'] == ['*circles*']:
        # post is public to all followed users; post is visible
        return True
    for circle in post['circles']:
        if circle in circles_user_is_in:
            # User is in a circle receiving this post
            return True
    return False
```

In order to quickly retrieve the pages in the desired order, we'll need an index on user_id, month in both the social.news and social.wall collections.

```
>>> for collection in ('db.social.news', 'db.social.wall'):
...     collection.ensure_index([
...         ('user_id', 1),
...         ('month', -1)])
```

Commenting on a Post

Other than viewing walls and news feeds, creating new posts is the next most common action taken on social networks. To create a comment by user on a given post containing the given text, we'll need to execute code similar to the following:

```
from datetime import datetime

def comment(user, post_id, text):
    ts = datetime.utcnow()
    month = ts.strfime('%Y%m')
    comment = {
        'by': { 'id': user['id'], 'name': user['name'] }
        'ts': ts,
        'text': text }
    # Update the social.posts collection
    db.social.post.update(
        { '_id': post_id },
        { '$push': { 'comments': comment } } )
```

```
# Update social.wall and social.news collections
db.social.wall.update(
    { 'posts.id': post_id },
    { '$push': { 'comments': comment },
      '$inc': { 'comments_shown': 1 } },
    upsert=True,
    multi=True)
db.social.news.update(
    { 'posts.id': _id },
    { '$push': { 'comments': comment },
      '$inc': { 'comments_shown': 1 } },
    upsert=True,
    multi=True)
```

The preceding code can actually result in an unbounded number of comments being inserted into the social.wall and social.news collections. To compensate for this, we need to periodically run the following update statement to truncate the number of displayed comments and keep the size of the news and wall documents manageable:

```
COMMENTS_SHOWN = 3

def truncate_extra_comments():
    db.social.news.update(
        { 'posts.comments_shown': { '$gt': COMMENTS_SHOWN } },
        { '$pop': { 'posts.$.comments': -1 },
          '$inc': { 'posts.$.comments_shown': -1 } },
        multi=True)
    db.social.wall.update(
        { 'posts.comments_shown': { '$gt': COMMENTS_SHOWN } },
        { '$pop': { 'posts.$.comments': -1 },
          '$inc': { 'posts.$.comments_shown': -1 } },
        multi=True)
```

In order to efficiently execute the updates to the social.news and social.wall collections just shown, we need to be able to quickly locate both of the following document types:

- Documents containing a given post
- Documents containing posts displaying too many comments

To quickly execute these updates, then, we need to create the following indexes:

```
>>> for collection in (db.social.news, db.social.wall):
...     collection.ensure_index('posts.id')
...     collection.ensure_index('posts.comments_shown')
```

Creating a New Post

Creating a new post fills out the content-creation activities on a social network:

```
from datetime import datetime

def post(user, dest_user, type, detail, circles):
    ts = datetime.utcnow()
    month = ts.strfime('%Y%m')
    post = {
        'ts': ts,
        'by': { id: user['id'], name: user['name'] },
        'circles': circles,
        'type': type,
        'detail': detail,
        'comments': [] }
    # Update global post collection
    db.social.post.insert(post)
    # Copy to dest user's wall
    if user['id'] not in dest_user['blocked']:
        append_post(db.social.wall, [dest_user['id']], month, post)
    # Copy to followers' news feeds
    if circles == ['*public*']:
        dest_userids = set(user['followers'].keys())
    else:
        dest_userids = set()
        if circles == [ '*circles*' ]:
            circles = user['circles'].keys()
        for circle in circles:
            dest_userids.update(user['circles'][circle])
    append_post(db.social.news, dest_userids, month, post)
```

The basic sequence of operations in this code is as follows:

1. The post is first saved into the "system of record," the social.post collection.

2. The recipient's wall is updated with the post.

3. The news feeds of everyone who is *circled* in the post is updated with the post.

Updating a particular wall or group of news feeds is then accomplished using the append_post function:

```
def append_post(collection, dest_userids, month, post):
    collection.update(
        { 'user_id': { '$in': sorted(dest_userids) },
          'month': month },
        { '$push': { 'posts': post } },
        multi=True)
```

In order to quickly update the social.wall and social.news collections, we once again need an index on both user_id and month. This time, however, the ideal order on the indexes is month, user_id. This is due to the fact that updates to these collections will always be for the current month; having month appear first in the index makes the index *right-aligned*, requiring significantly less memory to store the active part of the index.

However, in this case, since we already have an index `user_id`, `month`, which *must* be in that order to enable sorting on `month`, adding a second index is unnecessary, and would end up actually using more RAM to maintain two indexes. So even though this particular operation would benefit from having an index on `month`, `user_id`, it's best to leave out any additional indexes here.

Maintaining the Social Graph

In a social network, maintaining the social graph is an infrequent but essential operation. To add a user `other` to the current user `self`'s circles, we'll need to run the following function:

```python
def circle_user(self, other, circle):
    circles_path = 'circles.%s.%s' % (circle, other['_id'])
    db.social.user.update(
        { '_id': self['_id'] },
        { '$set': { circles_path: { 'name': other['name' ]} } })
    follower_circles = 'followers.%s.circles' % self['_id']
    follower_name = 'followers.%s.name' % self['_id']
    db.social.user.update(
        { '_id': other['_id'] },
        { '$push': { follower_circles: circle },
          '$set': { follower_name: self['name'] } })
```

Note that in this solution, previous posts of the `other` user are not added to the `self` user's news feed or wall. To actually include these past posts would be an expensive and complex operation, and goes beyond the scope of this use case.

Of course, we must also support *removing* users from circles:

```python
def uncircle_user(self, other, circle):
    circles_path = 'circles.%s.%s' % (circle, other['_id'])
    db.social.user.update(
        { '_id': self['_id'] },
        { '$unset': { circles_path: 1 } })
    follower_circles = 'followers.%s.circles' % self['_id']
    db.social.user.update(
        { '_id': other['_id'] },
        { '$pull': { follower_circles: circle } })
    # Special case -- 'other' is completely uncircled
    db.social.user.update(
        { '_id': other['_id'], follower_circles: {'$size': 0 } },
        { '$unset': { 'followers.' + self['_id' } }})
```

In both the circling and uncircling cases, the `_id` is included in the update queries, so no additional indexes are required.

Sharding

In order to scale beyond the capacity of a single replica set, we need to shard each of the collections mentioned previously. Since the social.user, social.wall, and so cial.news collections contain documents that are specific to a given user, the user's _id field is an appropriate shard key:

```
>>> db.command('shardcollection', 'dbname.social.user', {
...      'key': {'_id': 1 } } )
{ "collectionsharded": "dbname.social.user", "ok": 1 }
>>> db.command('shardcollection', 'dbname.social.wall', {
...      'key': {'user_id': 1 } } )
{ "collectionsharded": "dbname.social.wall", "ok": 1 }
>>> db.command('shardcollection', 'dbname.social.news', {
...      'key': {'user_id': 1 } } )
{ "collectionsharded": "dbname.social.news", "ok": 1 }
```

It turns out that using the posting user's _id is actually *not* the best choice for a shard key for social.post. This is due to the fact that queries and updates to this table are done using the _id field, and sharding on by.id, while tempting, would require these updates to be *broadcast* to all shards. To shard the social.post collection on _id, then, we need to execute the following command:

```
>>> db.command('shardcollection', 'dbame.social.post', {
... 'key': {'_id':1 } } )
{ "collectionsharded": "dbname.social.post", "ok": 1 }
```

## CHAPTER 9

Online Gaming

This chapter outlines the basic patterns and principles for using MongoDB as a persistent storage engine for an online game, particularly one that contains role-playing characteristics.

Solution Overview

In designing an online game, there is a need to store various data about the player's character. Some of the attributes might include:

Character attributes

> These might include intrinsic characteristics such as strength, dexterity, charisma, etc., as well as variable characteristics such as health, mana (if the game includes magic), etc.

Character inventory

> If our game includes the ability for the player to carry around objects, we'll need to keep track of the items carried.

Character location/relationship to the game world

> If our game allows the player to move their character from one location to another, this information needs to be stored as well.

In addition, we need to store all this data for large numbers of players who might be playing the game simultaneously, and this data needs to be both readable and writable with minimal latency in order to ensure responsiveness during gameplay.

In addition to the preceding data, we also need to store data for:

Items

> These include various artifacts that the character might interact with such as weapons, armor, treasure, etc.

Locations

The various locations in which characters and items might find themselves such as rooms, halls, etc.

Another consideration when designing the persistence backend for an online game is its flexibility. Particularly in early releases of a game, we might wish to change gameplay mechanics significantly as players provide feedback. When implementing these changes, being able to migrate persistent data from one format to another with minimal (or no) downtime is essential.

The solution presented by this use case assumes that the read and write performance is equally important and must be accessible with minimal latency.

Schema Design

Ultimately, the particulars of the schema depend on the design of the game. When designing our schema, we'll try to encapsulate all the commonly used data into a small number of objects in order to minimize the number of queries to the database and the number of seeks in a query. Encapsulating all player state into a character collection, item data into an item collection, and location data into a location collection satisfies both these criteria.

Character Schema

In a role-playing game, then, a typical character state document might look like the following:

```
{
    _id: ObjectId('...'),
    name: 'Tim',
    character: {
        intrinsics: {
            strength: 10,
            dexterity: 16,
            intelligence: 17,
            charisma: 8 },
        'class': 'mage',
        health: 212,
        mana: 152
    },
    location: {
        id: 'maze-1',
        description: 'a maze of twisty little passages...',
    exits: {n:'maze-2', s:'maze-1', e:'maze-3'},
        players: [
            { id:ObjectId('...'), name:'grue' },
            { id:ObjectId('...'), name:'Tim' }
            ],
```

```
        inventory: [
            { qty:1, id:ObjectId('...'), name:'scroll of cause fear' }]
        },
        gold: 523,
        armor: [
            { id:ObjectId('...'), region:'head'},
        { id:ObjectId('...'), region:'body'},
        { id:ObjectId('...'), region:'feet'}],
        weapons: [ {id:ObjectId('...'), hand:'both'} ],
        inventory: [
            { qty:1, id:ObjectId('...'), name:'backpack', inventory: [
                { qty:4, id:ObjectId('...'), name: 'potion of healing'},
            { qty:1, id:ObjectId('...'), name: 'scroll of magic mapping'},
                { qty:2, id:ObjectId('...'), name: 'c-rations'} ]},
            { qty:1, id:ObjectId('...'), name:"wizard's hat", bonus:3},
        { qty:1, id:ObjectId('...'), name:"wizard's robe", bonus:0},
        { qty:1, id:ObjectId('...'), name:"old boots", bonus:0},
        { qty:1, id:ObjectId('...'), name:"quarterstaff", bonus:2} ]
    }
```

There are a few things to note about this document:

- Information about the character's location in the game is encapsulated under the location attribute. Note in particular that all of the information necessary to describe the room is encapsulated within the character state document. This allows the game system to render the room without making a second query to the database to get room information.

- The armor and weapons attributes contain little information about the actual items being worn or carried. This information is actually stored under the inventory property. Since the inventory information is stored in the same document, there is no need to replicate the detailed information about each item into the armor and weapons properties.

- The inventory contains the item details necessary for rendering each item in the character's possession, including any enchantments (bonus) and quantity. Once again, embedding this data into the character record means we don't have to perform a separate query to fetch item details necessary for display.

Item Schema

Likewise, the item schema should include all details about all items globally in the game:

```
{
    _id: ObjectId('...'),
    name: 'backpack',
    bonus: null,
    inventory: [
        { qty:4, id:ObjectId('...'), name: 'potion of healing'},
```

```
       { qty:1, id:ObjectId('...'), name: 'scroll of magic mapping'},
          { qty:2, id:ObjectId('...'), name: 'c-rations'} ]},
     weight: 12,
     price: 160,
     ...
  }
```

Note that this document contains more or less the same information as stored in the `inventory` attribute of `character` documents, as well as additional data that may only be needed sporadically in the case of gameplay such as `weight` and `price`.

Location Schema

Finally, the `location` schema specifies the state of the world in the game:

```
  {
     id: 'maze-1',
     description: 'a maze of twisty little passages...',
     exits: {n:'maze-2', s:'maze-1', e:'maze-3'},
     players: [
        { id:ObjectId('...'), name:'grue' },
        { id:ObjectId('...'), name:'Tim' } ],
     inventory: [
        { qty:1, id:ObjectId('...'), name:'scroll of cause fear' } ],
  }
```

Here, note that `location` stores exactly the same information as is stored in the `location` attribute of the `character` document. We'll use `location` as the system of record when the game requires interaction between multiple characters or between characters and noninventory items.

Operations

In an online gaming system, with the state embedded in a single document for `character`, `item`, and `location`, the primary operations we'll be performing are as follows:

- Querying for the character state by `_id`
- Extracting relevant data for display
- Updating various attributes about the character

This section describes procedures for performing these queries, extractions, and updates. In particular, we will avoid loading the `location` or `item` documents except when absolutely necessary.

Load Character Data from MongoDB

The most basic operation in this system is loading the character state:

```
>>> character = db.characters.find_one({'_id': character_id})
```

In this case, the default index that MongoDB supplies on the _id field is sufficient for good performance of this query.

Extract Armor and Weapon Data for Display

In order to save space, the character schema just described stores item details only in the inventory attribute, storing ObjectIds in other locations. To display these item details, as on a character summary window, we need to merge the information from the armor and weapons attributes with information from the inventory attribute.

Suppose, for instance, that our code is displaying the armor data using the following Jinja2 template:

```
<div>
  <h2>Armor</h2>
  <dl>
    {% if value.head %}
      <dt>Helmet</dt>
      <dd>{{value.head[0].description}}</dd>
    {% endif %}
    {% if value.hands %}
      <dt>Gloves</dt>
      <dd>{{value.hands[0].description}}</dd>
    {% endif %}
    {% if value.feet %}
      <dt>Boots</dt>
      <dd>{{value.feet[0].description}}</dd>
    {% endif %}
    {% if value.body %}
      <dt>Body Armor</dt>
      <dd><ul>{% for piece in value.body %}
        <li>piece.description</li>
      {% endfor %}</ul></dd>
    {% endif %}
  </dl>
</dd>
```

In this case, we want the various description fields to be text similar to "+3 wizard's hat." The context passed to this template, then, would be of the following form:

```
{
    "head": [ { "id":..., "description": "+3 wizard's hat" } ],
    "hands": [],
    "feet": [ { "id":..., "description": "old boots" } ],
    "body": [ { "id":..., "description": "wizard's robe" } ],
}
```

In order to build up this structure, we'll use the following helper functions:

```python
def get_item_index(inventory):
    '''Given an inventory attribute, recursively build up an item
    index (including all items contained within other items)
    '''

    result = {}
    for item in inventory:
        result[item['_id']] = item
        if 'inventory' in item:
            result.update(get_item_index(item['inventory']))
    return result

def describe_item(item):
    '''Add a 'description' field to the given item'''

    result = dict(item)
    if item['bonus']:
        description = '%+d %s' % (item['bonus'], item['name'])
    else:
        description = item['name']
    result['description'] = description
    return result

def get_armor_for_display(character, item_index):
    '''Given a character document, return an 'armor' value
    suitable for display'''

    result = dict(head=[], hands=[], feet=[], body=[])
    for piece in character['armor']:
        item = describe_item(item_index[piece['id']])
        result[piece['region']].append(item)
    return result
```

In order to actually display the armor, then, we'd use the following code:

```python
>>> item_index = get_item_index(
...     character['inventory'] + character['location']['inventory'])
>>> armor = get_armor_for_dislay(character, item_index)
```

Note in particular that we're building an index not only for the items the character is actually carrying in inventory, but also for the items that the player might interact with in the room.

Similarly, in order to display the weapon information, we need to build a structure such as the following:

```
{
    "left": None,
    "right": None,
    "both": { "description": "+2 quarterstaff" }
}
```

The helper function is similar to that for `get_armor_for_display`:

```
def get_weapons_for_display(character, item_index):
    '''Given a character document, return a 'weapons' value
    suitable for display'''

    result = dict(left=None, right=None, both=None)
    for piece in character['weapons']:
        item = describe_item(item_index[piece['id']])
        result[piece['hand']] = item
    return result
```

In order to actually display the weapons, then, we'd use the following code:

```
>>> armor = get_weapons_for_display(character, item_index)
```

Extract Character Attributes, Inventory, and Room Information for Display

In order to display information about the character's attributes, inventory, and surroundings, we also need to extract fields from the character state. In this case, however, the schema just defined keeps all the relevant information for display embedded in those sections of the document. The code for extracting this data, then, is the following:

```
>>> attributes = character['character']
>>> inventory = character['inventory']
>>> room_data = character['location']
```

Pick Up an Item from a Room

In our game, suppose the player decides to pick up an item from the room and add it to their inventory. In this case, we need to update both the character state and the global location state:

```
def pick_up_item(character, item_index, item_id):
    '''Transfer an item from the current room to the character's inventory'''

    item = item_index[item_id]
    character['inventory'].append(item)
    db.character.update(
        { '_id': character['_id'] },
        { '$push': { 'inventory': item },
          '$pull': { 'location.inventory': { '_id': item['id'] } } })
```

```
db.location.update(
    { '_id': character['location']['id'] },
    { '$pull': { 'inventory': { 'id': item_id } } })
```

While the preceding code may be for a single-player game, if we allow multiple players or nonplayer characters to pick up items, that introduces a problem where two characters may try to pick up an item simultaneously. To guard against that, we can use the location collection to decide between ties. In this case, the code is now the following:

```
def pick_up_item(character, item_index, item_id):
    '''Transfer an item from the current room to the character's inventory'''

    item = item_index[item_id]
    character['inventory'].append(item)
    result = db.location.update(
        { '_id': character['location']['id'],
          'inventory.id': item_id },
        { '$pull': { 'inventory': { 'id': item_id } } },
        safe=True)
    if not result['updatedExisting']:
        raise Conflict()
    db.character.update(
        { '_id': character['_id'] },
        { '$push': { 'inventory': item },
          '$pull': { 'location': { '_id': item['id'] } } })
```

By ensuring that the item is present before removing it from the room in the update call, we guarantee that only one player/nonplayer character/monster can pick up the item.

Remove an Item from a Container

In the game described here, the backpack item can contain other items. We might further suppose that some other items may be similarly hierarchical (e.g., a chest in a room). Suppose that the player wishes to move an item from one of these "containers" into their active inventory as a prelude to using it. In this case, we need to update both the character state and the item state:

```
def move_to_active_inventory(character, item_index, container_id, item_id):
    '''Transfer an item from the given container to the character's active
    inventory
    '''

    result = db.item.update( ❶
        { '_id': container_id,
          'inventory.id': item_id },
        { '$pull': { 'inventory': { 'id': item_id } } },
        safe=True)
    if not result['updatedExisting']:
        raise Conflict()
    item = item_index[item_id]
```

```
    container = item_index[item_id]
    character['inventory'].append(item) ❷
    container['inventory'] = [ ❸
        item for item in container['inventory']
        if item['_id'] != item_id ]
    db.character.update( ❹
        { '_id': character['_id'] },
        { '$push': { 'inventory': item } } )
    db.character.update( ❺
        { '_id': character['_id'], 'inventory.id': container_id },
        { '$pull': { 'inventory.$.inventory': { 'id': item_id } } } )
```

Note in this code that we:

❶ Ensure that the item's state makes this update reasonable (the item is actually contained within the container). Abort with an error if this is not true.

❷ Update the in-memory character document's inventory, adding the item.

❸ Update the in-memory container document's inventory, removing the item.

❹ Update the character document in MongoDB.

❺ In the case that the character is moving an item from a container *in his own inventory*, update the character's inventory representation of the container.

Move the Character to a Different Room

In our game, suppose the player decides to move north. In this case, we need to update the character state to match the new location:

```
def move(character, direction):
    '''Move the character to a new location'''

    # Remove character from current location
    db.location.update(
        {'_id': character['location']['id'] },
        {'$pull': {'players': {'id': character['_id'] } } })
    # Add character to new location, retrieve new location data
    new_location = db.location.find_and_modify(
        { '_id': character['location']['exits'][direction] },
        { '$push': { 'players': {
            'id': character['_id'],
            'name': character['name'] } } },
        new=True)
    character['location'] = new_location
    db.character.update(
        { '_id': character['_id'] },
        { '$set': { 'location': new_location } })
```

Here, note that the code updates the old room, the new room, and the character document. Since we're using $push and $pull operations to update the location collection, we don't need to worry about race conditions.

Buy an Item

If the character wants to buy an item, we need to do the following:

1. Add that item to the character's inventory.

2. Decrement the character's gold.

3. Increment the shopkeeper's gold.

4. Update the room.

The following code does just that:

```python
def buy(character, shopkeeper, item_id):
    '''Pick up an item, add to the character's inventory, and transfer
    payment to the shopkeeper
    '''

    price = db.item.find_one({'_id': item_id}, {'price':1})['price']
    result = db.character.update(
        { '_id': character['_id'],
          'gold': { '$gte': price } },
        { '$inc': { 'gold': -price } },
        safe=True )
    if not result['updatedExisting']:
        raise InsufficientFunds()
    try:
        pick_up_item(character, item_id)
    except:
        # Add the gold back to the character
        result = db.character.update(
            { '_id': character['_id'] },
            { '$inc': { 'gold': price } } )
        raise
    character['gold'] -= price
    db.character.update(
        { '_id': shopkeeper['_id'] },
        { '$inc': { 'gold': price } } )
```

Note that the buy() function ensures that the character has sufficient gold to pay for the item using the updatedExisting trick used for picking up items. The race condition for item pickup is handled as well, "rolling back" the removal of gold from the character's wallet if the item cannot be picked up.

Why so much application code?

If you're coming from a relational database, particularly if you have a background as a DBA, you may be accustomed to pushing as much logic as possible into the database. Although this approach may be desirable in some circumstances, it's really not feasible with MongoDB due to limited programming capabilities within the server (compared to many relational database systems). Moving more of the workload to the application servers, as MongoDB often requires, actually carries with it an important benefit: application servers are typically *much* easier to scale than database servers. Even with MongoDB's straightforward sharding, it's hard to compete with the scale-up sequence for an app server:

1. Bring up an app server
2. Add it to the load balancer

Of course, there are some cases where data locality and indexes can make doing some operations on the MongoDB server more efficient. A good rule of thumb is to consider whether there's a significant performance advantage to keeping a calculation on the MongoDB server, and if not, move it to the application layer.

Sharding

If the system needs to scale beyond a single MongoDB node, we'll want to use a sharded cluster. Sharding in this use case is fairly straightforward, since all our items are always retrieved by _id. To shard the `character` and `location` collections, the commands would be the following:

```
>>> db.command('shardcollection', 'dbname.character', {
...     'key': { '_id': 1 } })
{ "collectionsharded" : "dbname.character", "ok" : 1 }
>>> db.command('shardcollection', 'dbname.location', {
...     'key': { '_id': 1 } })
{ "collectionsharded" : "dbname.location", "ok" : 1 }
```

Afterword

In this book, you've seen some common design patterns used with MongoDB applications:

- Embedding subdocuments versus referencing them by _id
- Using MongoDB's dynamic schemas to enable polymorphic data
- Methods of mimicking transactions with a nontransactional database

You've also seen examples of how you might apply these design patterns in various scenarios:

- Real-time analytics
- Ecommerce
- Content management systems
- Online advertising
- Social networking
- Online gaming

The truth, of course, is that the world of NoSQL, and particularly MongoDB, is exploding right now. No book can hope to be a comprehensive catalog of schema design, operational architecture, sharding, and replication setup. My hope is that this book has given you a flavor for the kinds of decisions you're going to have to make in your own applications. By seeing concrete examples of problems and good MongoDB solutions, you should be able to extend the approaches here to the particular problems you face.

Where Do I Go from Here?

Some of the best sources for ongoing MongoDB education and networking are the MongoDB conference series and user groups. 10gen (the MongoDB company) hosts one-day conferences, sometimes accompanied by training workshops, in various cities around the world. For a list of conferences, some of the meetups, as well as other upcoming events, you can visit 10gen's Events and Webinars page (*http://10gen.com/ events*).

Additionally, several of the use cases in this book can also be found in the MongoDB Manual's Use Cases section (*http://docs.mongodb.org/manual/use-cases/*), along with a wealth of additional documentation.

We have a web page for this book, where we list errata, examples, and any additional information. You can access this page at *http://oreil.ly/mongodb-applied-design-patterns*.

To comment or ask technical questions about this book, send email to *bookques tions@oreilly.com*.

Index

Symbols

2, 82

A

ad serving, 121–124
  algorithm for, 121
ad zones, 121
$addToSet operator, 107
adding and removing friends, 138
ad_iterator generator, 126, 127
aggregation framework, 45
aggregation pipeline, 45
ALTER TABLE statement, 20
append_post function, 137
armor attribute, 143, 145
array of properties approach, 23
arrays, 3, 8
artifacts in online games, 141
asset management (see content storage in CMS)
atomic multistatement transactions, 26
autoincrement primary key, 65
automatic sharding, 10, 48

B

B-tree structure, 44
base64-encoding, 130
batch inserts, 42

bidirectional connections, 130
BLOB data, 4, 78
blobs of binary data, 103
blogs and blog posts, 101, 110
breadcrumb navigation, 86
BSON document format, 3, 8, 21, 38
bson.ObjectId(), 100
bulk inserts, 42
buy() function, 150

C

capped collections, 51
carted attribute, 95
category hierarchy (see product categories)
character data in online gaming, 141, 142, 145, 147
choose_ad() call, 126
chunks, 48
chunk_size, 107
circles property, 131, 135
cleanup operations, 32, 98
CMS (content management systems)
  comment storage, 111–120
  content storage, 101–111
collections
  capped, 51
  dependent, 132
  for GridFS data, 103
  in MongoDB, 11

We'd like to hear your suggestions for improving our indexes. Send email to index@oreilly.com.

GridFS, 103, 107
$group operator, 46
group commits, 41
$gte conditional, 43

H

hashes, 48
helper function, 87, 146
hierarchical aggregated reports
    operations for, 67–72
    schema design, 65
    sharding, 72
    solution overview, 64
hierarchical classification (see product categories)
hierarchical documents, 56
hint(), 45
historical charts, 62
hourly field, 54
hourly statistics, 67
h_aggregate function, 72

I

_id field, 14, 46, 102
$inc modifier, 95, 117
incomplete write operations, 9
increment operation, 53
independent collections, 130
indexes
    case sensitivity of, 82
    for accelerating queries, 83
    managing size of, 42
    RAM usage, 42, 138
    right-aligned, 43, 137
    rules for design of, 44
    unique, 110
inheritance, 17
insert(), 42, 113
inserting log records, 39
inventory attribute, 145
inventory management
    operations for, 93–99
    schema design, 92
    sharding for, 100
    solution overview, 91
inventory property, 143
isolation levels, 10

items in online games
    picking up, 147
    purchasing, 150
    removing, 148
    storing data for, 141, 143

J

j (journal) option, 41
JavaScript lock, 66
join collection query, 13
JOIN operation, 6, 77
JSON (JavaScript Object Notation) format, 8

K

key columns, 6
key-value pairs, 8
keyword targeting, 126–128
keywords, 126

L

last_run variable, 67, 69, 72
limit(), 12
list function, 89
location in online gaming, 141, 143, 144, 149
locked field, 108
$lt operator, 43
$lte operator, 134

M

many-to-many (M:N) relationships, 13
mapf function, 66
MapReduce, 65
mapreduce command, 63, 64
$match operation, 46, 48
media sites, 121
metadata management (see content storage in CMS)
migration scripts, 20
Ming, 21
minute property, 55
mongod, 84, 100
MongoDB
    aggregation framework, 45
    arrays of data in, 3
    atomic update operations in, 25, 28, 33
    automatic sharding, 10
    benefits and complications of, 8

$set modifier, 95
shard clusters, 48, 151
shard keys
    compound, 50, 72, 124
    files_id field, 110
    hashes, 48
    in MongoDB, 48
    node_id, 119
    path field, 49
    selecting, 50
    semi-random, 49
    slug or full slug, 119
    three-part, 63
    timestamps, 48
    type field, 83
    unique indexes, 110
    user_id, 139
    _id field, 100, 126
shardcollection command, 63, 83
sharding
    ad serving, 124
    automatic, 10, 48
    CMS comment storage, 119
    CMS content storage, 110
    event data, 48–50
    frequency capping, 126
    hierarchical aggregated reports, 72
    inventory management, 100
    online gaming, 151
    pre-aggregated reports, 63
    product catalogs, 83
    product categories, 90
    social networking, 139
shopping carts (see online shopping carts)
short_description field, 22
site_id, 121, 123, 126
$size query, 133
skip(), 12
$slice operator, 116
slug field, 86, 102
social graphs, 129, 138
social networking
    operations for, 133–138
    schema design, 130–133
    sharding for, 139
    solution overview, 129
SQL equivalent statements, 47
status updates, 129
$sum statement, 46

T

this keyword, 66
threaded comments, 114, 116
time field, 47
time to live (TTL) indexes, 51
timestamps, 38, 48
transactional data, 37, 63
ts (timestamp) value, 67
TTL collections, 51
two-phase commit protocol, 26, 30
txn_id, 32
type field, 83
types, using proper, 38

U

uncapped collections, 37
update() statement, 29
updates
    atomic, 14
    complex, 28
    emulating transactions, 30–33
    in relational databases, 26
    incomplete write operations, 9
    optimistic with compensation, 29–33
    speed of, 13, 53, 83
uploading photos, 107
upsert operation, 53, 54, 57, 59
user comments (see comments)
user profiles, 124, 129
user_id, 126
UTCtimestamp, 38

V

viewing paginated comments, 113, 116, 118

W

wall posts, 134
weapons attribute, 143, 145
web pages, 101
weekly statistics, 70
write concern, 40

Z

zone_id, 121, 123, 126

About the Author

Rick Copeland is the principal consultant and founder of Arborian Consulting, a business focusing on MongoDB and Python custom development and training. Rick is a frequent speaker at MongoDB events, an avid MongoDB enthusiast, and a charter member of 10gen's "MongoDB Masters." On the non-MongoDB side of things, Rick is also a well-known Python developer and member of the Python Software Foundation, having contributed to a number of open source projects and spoken at various events and user groups.

Rick is also the author of *Essential SQLAlchemy* (O'Reilly), which introduces readers to the excellent SQLAlchemyPython database toolkit.

Colophon

The animal on the cover of *MongoDB Applied Design Patterns* is the thirteen-lined ground squirrel (*Ictidomys tridecemlineatus*), also known as the leopard ground squirrel, squinney, or striped gopher. It gains both its Latin name (*tredecim* meaning thirteen) and common name from the 13 alternating dark and light lines that run down its back and sides. It also has spots within the darker stripes of fur, which help camouflage the animal in its grassland habitat.

Thirteen-lined ground squirrels are widespread in the Great Plains region of North America, and in fact are the reason for Minnesota's nickname "The Gopher State" (though this is a misnomer, as they are not members of the gopher family). Strictly active during the day, this squirrel's diet consists of grass, seeds, and insects. They prefer open areas with short grass and well-drained soil for creating their burrows. Though they live individually rather than in colonies, there may be as many as 20 ground squirrels per acre in a particularly good habitat.

These animals range from 6–11 inches long, and their weight varies widely depending on the time of year. Most usually weigh between 5–6 ounces, but can get near half a pound when preparing for winter hibernation. In preparation, the ground squirrel puts on a heavy layer of fat and stores food in its burrow. Around October, it enters the burrow, rolls into a tight ball, and decreases its respiration to about one breath every five minutes, until it emerges again in March or April.

Each thirteen-lined ground squirrel's burrow is around 15–20 feet long, with several side passages and multiple entrances. With the exception of the hibernation chamber, the burrows are no more than 1-2 feet below the surface. Typically, the tunnel turns sharply near its beginning, to trick digging predators into believing that the burrow has dead-ended.

The cover image is from Wood's *Animate Creation*. The cover font is Adobe ITC Garamond. The text font is Adobe Minion Pro; the heading font is Adobe Myriad Condensed; and the code font is Dalton Maag's Ubuntu Mono.

Have it your way.

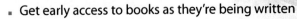

Get even more for your money.

Join the O'Reilly Community, and register the O'Reilly books you own. It's free, and you'll get:

- $4.99 ebook upgrade offer
- 40% upgrade offer on O'Reilly print books
- Membership discounts on books and events
- Free lifetime updates to ebooks and videos
- Multiple ebook formats, DRM FREE
- Participation in the O'Reilly community
- Newsletters
- Account management
- 100% Satisfaction Guarantee

Signing up is easy:

1. **Go to: oreilly.com/go/register**
2. **Create an O'Reilly login.**
3. **Provide your address.**
4. **Register your books.**

Note: English-language books only

To order books online:
oreilly.com/store

For questions about products or an order:
orders@oreilly.com

To sign up to get topic-specific email announcements and/or news about upcoming books, conferences, special offers, and new technologies:
elists@oreilly.com

For technical questions about book content:
booktech@oreilly.com

To submit new book proposals to our editors:
proposals@oreilly.com

O'Reilly books are available in multiple DRM-free ebook formats. For more information:
oreilly.com/ebooks

O'REILLY®

Spreading the knowledge of innovators   oreilly.com

Lightning Source UK Ltd.
Milton Keynes UK
UKOW022120020413

208530UK00002B/5/P